THINKING IN PLACE

Cultural Politics & the Promise of Democracy
A Series from Paradigm Publishers
Edited by Henry A. Giroux

⊸

THINKING IN PLACE
ART, ACTION, AND CULTURAL PRODUCTION

CAROL BECKER

Paradigm Publishers
Boulder • London

Copyright © 2009 Paradigm Publishers

Published in the United States by Paradigm Publishers, 3360 Mitchell Lane, Suite E, Boulder, CO 80301, USA.

Paradigm Publishers is the trade name of Birkenkamp & Company, LLC, Dean Birkenkamp, President and Publisher.

Library of Congress Cataloging-in-Publication Data

Becker, Carol.
    Thinking in place : art, action, and cultural production / Carol Becker.
        p. cm.
    Includes bibliographical references.
    ISBN-13: 978-1-59451-596-5 (hardcover : alk. paper)
    1. Place (Philosophy) in art. 2. Place (Philosophy). 3. Arts. 4. Becker, Carol.
    I. Title.
    NX650.P52B43 2008
    700.1—dc22
                                                                    2008015131

Printed and bound in the United States of America on acid-free paper that meets the standards of the American National Standard for Permanence of Paper for Printed Library Materials.

Designed and typeset by Straight Creek Bookmakers.

13 12 11 10 09   1 2 3 4 5

For my mother, Helen Becker, 1908–2005,

in love and gratitude

Contents

⟿

Acknowledgments

꩜

I have chosen my friends and colleagues with great care. Their goodwill, enthusiasm, brilliance, creativity, and commitment to social change have helped me to think through complex issues and to have faith in my own version of how to approach them. Their passions and accomplishments inspire me daily. I am grateful to Lin Hixson, Matthew Goulish, Adrian Heathfield, Roberta Lynch, Judith Raphael, Alda Blanco, Susanna Coffey, Carole Wanghaw, Kathryn Sapoznick, Lisa Wainwright, Ernesto Pujol, Henry Giroux, Susan Searls, Jacobo Konigsberg, Andries Botha, Janine Antoni, Paul Ramirez Jonas, France Morin, Peter Murchie, Stephanie Farquhar, and, the newest addition to my family of friends, Sampson Farquhar Murchie.

All writers should have a wonderful architect partner willing to build them a perfect studio in the country so they can dream in solitude. Jack Murchie has been my own architect and life partner. I am grateful daily for his love and devotion.

My debt to the School of the Art Institute is apparent throughout these chapters. My many years as a faculty member and as dean of faculty taught me so much about how to look at and think about the process of art and design. Those understandings are manifested in many ideas presented in this collection. I am forever grateful to the faculty, staff, and students for all I learned from them individually and collectively and for the wild spirit of extraordinary creativity that enlivens that community.

My debt to my new home, Columbia University, is less obvious but is nonetheless essential. Columbia University and the School of the Arts have been very generous and trusting in affording me the time and resources to complete this book before moving to New York. It is a tribute to their own passion for ideas that they were willing to extend the time to me to complete this project. Thank you to the entire faculty and staff of the School of the Arts, and especially to Lee Bollinger, Nick Dirks, and Alan Brinkley.

Of course none of this would have worked if Jana Wright had not been willing to make the move with me to Columbia and had she not been more than capable of flying solo and launching our presence at the university in the fall of 2007. Her brilliance and stamina amaze me every day. I wish us many more great years of collaboration, innovation, and friendship together.

Andrea Uptmor, my brilliant, talented assistant for the last years at the School of the Art Institute, has helped me structure all the images for my speaking presentations as well as for this book. Joey Orr, my research assistant, found fabulous information. He jumped into each project with an open heart and mind. It has been my pleasure to work with these profoundly intelligent and creative young people who have treated my project as their own. It is a joy to have known them at this time of their lives and to be assured that they will go on to be stars in the worlds of their choice.

Janet Kaplan and Patricia Phillips, in their role as *Art Journal* editors, encouraged innovation in form and published early versions of some of these chapters.

My editor Jean Fulton returned to assist me with the completion of this book. She has sharpened the thinking and writing of each chapter with her intelligent queries and concerns. She has been a wonderful, compassionate editor, and foremost a loyal friend.

Henry Giroux once again believed in me enough to encourage this book and to make a place for it in his own series. He continues to inspire me with his passion for ideas and for social justice. Thank you also to Dean Birkenkamp and to Paradigm Publishers for all their assistance in seeing the book through to completion.

I lost my mother, Helen Becker, three years ago. She was almost ninety-eight years old, yet clear of mind and spirit. Her tenacity, wisdom, beauty, and savvy brought me a great deal of joy, especially in our last years together. It is to her and to the force that she continues to represent in my life that I dedicate this book.

Prologue
Wandering Monks and Peripatetic Birds

⊸

> Memory, like the mind and time, is unimaginable without physical place to make it into a landscape in which its contents are located, and what has location can be approached.[1]

Thinking in Place: Art, Action, and Cultural Production is the result of the past decade of wandering. Many of my adventures have been a combination of play and purposefulness. I have traveled to teach, give keynote addresses, offer a series of lectures, work in collective projects, visit specific schools, take art students on study trips, or attempt to write in remote islands off the coast of northern Greece. I have also moved around the world simply to dream deeply in extraordinary locations in the hope that I would become more sophisticated about the complexity of culture and better able to evaluate the potential of the species to evolve.

In motion in these ways, I also have learned how it feels to be lost in language and space, caught in complex political dynamics and the negotiation of otherness. I have slept in very modest dwellings in villages in Africa and Latin America, and I have learned to be in the mix, enjoying daily life in such remote locations, while also stressed and made anxious by its uncertainties and instabilities like everyone else. I have also stayed in five-star French-owned hotels in the Mekong Delta and other locations, and learned the limitations of being so insulated that I felt as though I had not left home at all, except that in such places I could experience greater luxury than I ever might in Chicago. I have also learned how angry I can become when the opportunity for the experience of place is truncated, sanitized, or simply replaced by the nonspaces of homogenized, globalized society. These extremes have taught me a great deal about the complex anxiety we all can experience when leaving the familiar.

Many of the places to which I am drawn are difficult in that to be there is often to experience turmoil and at times a sense of danger. South Africa has been such a place, yet I have found great joy there, in the depth of the experiences I have had with people and with the sophistication of ideas that inevitably surround issues and debates.

But in all such encounters I have experienced the true joy of wandering—a state of mind and body of which I never seem to get enough. I attribute some of this voracious restlessness in me to the writer who is always hungry for unstructured time in which the mind, unfettered, unhinged from the contingencies of daily life, can think its own thoughts and roam freely in its own vastness.

This type of restlessness does not arise from a need to consume the world nor to complete a checklist of must-see places. A great deal of my restlessness involves acting on a desire to return, again and again, to locations where my experience has been profound, whether because of the sensual comfort and beauty of the place or because of the cultural complexity it has presented. When I cannot physically travel to these places, I often visit them in my mind. Some of these—South Africa, Laos, Cambodia, Vietnam—have now become so familiar that they draw me back repeatedly, literally and metaphorically.

Needing to retouch the atmosphere of a place in order to reawaken those feelings and thoughts that they have conjured is like the motion of migratory birds that travel the same flight each year and choose to rest for a time in the same locations—those that are convenient, comfortable, and certainly familiar. They then move on in flocks, making these seasonal elliptical orbits for the entirety of their lives, habits founded on necessity.

Wandering monks who move from temple to temple or monastery to monastery also do a bit of the same, visiting each site for days or even years at a time, never making any one place *the* place, no one community *the* community, yet living in each one fully during the time they are there.

There is a whole genre of travel now known as "trauma tourism," which involves the conscious choice to put oneself in very difficult situations. Although I have been to places that have been the location of serious conflict or unrest—the village of the My Lai massacre or Birla House where Gandhi was shot, for example—I never did enter into these experiences anticipating the extent of emotions they would unleash. I went there simply to pay homage, never intending at the time that I would later write about them.

Given my Jewish heritage, I avoided Germany for most of my adult life. When I was invited to participate in a conference in Berlin in 1995 to celebrate the role of the arts since World War II, I thought that perhaps this was the right time to go. As part of the weeklong events, they took us on the "Topography of Terror" tour. Among multiple sites we visited was Wannsee House, where, on January 20, 1942, the "Final Solution of the Jewish Question" was determined. Here I saw an exhibit of photographs taken by German soldiers during the war. On the surface the photos were not terribly sensational, except for the astonishing fact that these soldiers were documenting their own horrific acts. But one particular photo has haunted me for all these years. It was an image of a dark winter street covered in snow, dimly lit by gas lamps. A group of well-dressed German-Jewish men and women in dinner clothes—long coats with fur collars, high-heeled shoes—were walking in the middle of this frozen street at gunpoint, followed by young German soldiers. These people, with literally nothing but the coats on their backs, probably had no knowledge of where they were going, but perhaps instinctively knew that they were leaving everyone and everything they loved behind, forever. My immediate response to this image was so primal and terrifying that I began to hyperventilate and had to sit down. To this day I can conjure a sickening sense of desolation when I think of this exhibition and the Wannsee House itself as a location for a barbarous decision from which the world has still not recovered.

At times I have been curious to see how a horrific event such as this one has been represented in space, at its original location—the mix of information, historical contextualization, and emotional experience that the best sites have tried not to overorchestrate for their audiences. But mostly I have traveled because something from the inside has compelled me to a place on the outside, or someone has lured me to a situation and structured my participation in it. I often did not know these places would affect me as they did or that the only response would then be to spend months trying to organize my thoughts about them in writing. *Thinking in Place* embodies several such attempts to give form to these unexpected experiences.

At the same time that I am a wanderer, I also plant deep roots. I spent twenty-seven years at the School of the Art Institute of Chicago as a teacher and administrator, helping to build that wonderful institution. Its ethics and eccentricities have become part of my conscious and unconscious life. There and within the broader world of educating artists I learned to look at art and the nature of the creative process. During this time of staying put while also moving around the world, I truly began to understand what it means to position myself and my writing in a global context. I also began to think of what "the global" means and will mean for young creative practitioners.

I have had the joy of living my adult life around artists and designers, observing their methodology. And throughout the writing of the first chapters of this book, I have thought repeatedly of a quote by artist Robert Irwin, who, while preparing for a large exhibition in San Diego, told the interviewer, "An exhibition for me is not a statement but an experiment."[2] I like that he has been willing to use exhibitions as an opportunity to take risks in form and content. The past years of writing have been such for me as I've tried to mix memory, theory, historical fact, and metaphor, never quite sure the amalgam would hold.

Now brought together, these chapters make it apparent how each place has made me search for a unique form in writing to re-create its effect. I am hopeful that the passion I feel for each location and the ideas generated from each will be the connective tissue that will make the experience of these chapters cumulative.

I also sincerely wish that those more clever than I will continue to take up the issues with which I am concerned here—the pedagogy of artists and designers, racism, poverty, exploitation, ignorance, war, peace, and the human capacity to create beauty and to revel in it. I also hope that as a species we can recognize, with increased clarity, how important it is to support those capable of using art and ideas ingeniously, not only because such people entertain us with the outcomes of their obsessions, but because their hearts and minds have the capacity to transform the world and our understanding of it in unexpected ways.

Notes

1. Rebecca Solnit, *Wanderlust: A History of Walking* (New York: Penguin, 2000), 77.

2. Jori Finkel, "Artist of Light, Space and Now, Trees," *New York Times*, Arts and Leisure, October 14, 2007, 35.

I
Defining Place
Crown Heights and the Coal Mines
of Western Pennsylvania

✦

To my grandmothers, Catherine and Esther

Geography is mostly about how we strive to feel at home on Earth, rooted in place, yet ... we never quite succeed.[1]

One year after the 1991 riots in Crown Heights, Brooklyn, I brought my boyfriend Jack to visit the neighborhood for the first time. Before we even stepped out of the car, a police vehicle pulled up next to us and asked what we were doing there. I said I was showing this boy from northern Michigan the place where I grew up. My explanation satisfied them, and they drove on.

At the time it was Purim, a Jewish festival when children dress up in costumes. For some reason this particular year the streets were filled with small boys and girls in miniature bride and groom attire—boys in top hats, black jackets, white shirts, and ties; girls in frilly white dresses with veils. It looked like a group wedding in miniature.

The other young people on the street were dressed as chickens. Men from the Lubavitcher sect with yarmulkes and forelocks were running back and forth helping these children cross the street, and the neighborhood surely resembled a nineteenth-century Jewish ghetto, a *shtetl*. As we got out of the car, Jack, a bit stunned, turned to me and said, "You're right, you didn't grow up in America." But of course I did. This is what America, Brooklyn-style, looked like in the 1950s and, in many respects, it is what Crown Heights still looks like today.

This location marks the site of the early formative period of my life. It was here that the enormous issues of race, religion, and sectarianism entered my consciousness; that I first understood the nature of Otherness; and that I was asked to "choose" my affiliation—Jewish or Catholic? Later I developed my own eclectic spiritual practice, incorporating both religions as well as Buddhism. But in those days these polarizations were omnipresent and weighed profoundly on my consciousness. Still, I am grateful for my life among the many racial and ethnic groups of Crown Heights. This complexity made me curious and fearless about difference and prepared me for the diversity of U.S. society and for the travels inside and outside the United States that were to come.

Duality

My mother was a first-generation American of Polish-Catholic descent from Hastings, a small mining town in western Pennsylvania. She was the second oldest in a family of nine children. Her immigrant father was killed in the coal mines in 1919. And like so many other families in that region, hers was very poor. She needed to leave Hastings to earn money to help support them all. In 1923, when she was fifteen years old, she went to New York to seek employment, a practice not uncommon among youth in Pennsylvania mining towns at that time. It was here, later, that she met my father.

He was a first-generation American of Russian-Jewish parentage who grew up in Williamsburg, Brooklyn. His immigrant father was a tailor. There were six children. When he and my mother met he was a gambler—cards and dice. They were introduced by a common friend—a dancing partner of my mother's. Because my father quickly realized that my tall, blond, gorgeous mother was not Jewish, he told her that his last name was Cunningham. During their courtship she learned the truth. Hesitant more about the gambling than the religion, she waited a long time to marry him—ten years. A decade later and some time after the war ended, I was born.

As a result of this literally unorthodox union, I spent my childhood moving between the complexities of their two realities. Crown Heights was our primary residence. It was where I attended school. Hastings was the location of my grandmother's farm, where she lived with one of my many aunts and uncles. There in Hastings I spent my summers and most other vacations with my mother's family. These visits continued long after my grandmother died. In both localities I had a large extended family. In each I had a grandmother whom I adored who spoke very little English.

These two locations embodied the extreme differences of my parents. But the meanings embedded in them had even greater political gravitas so soon after World War II than I ever could have imagined as a child. To me, each place represented half of my identity. Between them I lived the complexity of urban and rural, Jewish and Catholic, Russian and Polish, peasant and working class.

Because I was of mixed religions, I was treated as an anomaly in the predominantly Jewish and Hasidic neighborhood of Crown Heights. Here I knew a few Catholics, but, unlike my family, they were all Italian. Although ours was the only family in my building to have a Christmas tree and to dye Easter eggs, I also studied Hebrew and observed the Jewish holidays with all my Jewish friends. I never understood, until I was much older, that according to Orthodox Jewish law I was not considered Jewish because my mother was not Jewish, and she had not chosen to convert.

Because I was from a dual-religion household, no small matter in those days, I was also treated as an anomaly in the very Catholic, provincial, rural setting of Hastings, Pennsylvania. On Sundays when my Polish cousins went to church, I stayed home with my mother. From time to time on holidays I also went to church, where they did speak English and not Polish, as many Pennsylvania Catholic churches did, to the dismay of Rome, but I never went to confession. When I did go, I was often horrified by the moral import of the sermons. I was spared such moral discourse in Brooklyn since the rabbis in the small Orthodox synagogue (*shul*) we all attended in Crown Heights (women upstairs, men downstairs) did not speak about politics, and, if they did, I would never have understood the Hebrew well enough to know it.

In comparison with Catholicism, Orthodox Judaism appeared bacchanalian—lots of raucous singing and dancing and festivals of the harvest. Because New York was the place I identified most as my home, it is also not surprising that I favored the religion of my friends and family there. But in attempting to choose one religion, I was aware that it appeared that I was choosing my father and his family over my mother and her family. For many years I placed rosary beads in my shoes. I'm sure this was in part because I was drawn to the suffering of Catholic saints, but also, and perhaps more significantly, because I felt some guilt about identifying as a Jew. It is also possible that I was just hedging my bets.

Another very dominant contradiction that I experienced was that of rural and urban. Although none of my friends in Brooklyn had had any contact with farm life, for me this was an essential part of my upbringing. Among my friends in that working-class Brooklyn neighborhood, only I went away for two months in the summers to a farm. Some people rented bungalows in Rockaway for a week or two, some families went to the Catskills, but most did not venture anywhere other than the stoop in front of our building, nor had they the money or opportunity to do so. (If they did have an extended family, they probably lived close.) Only I had milked cows, planted crops, fed pigs, ridden horses, shoveled manure, and bailed hay as part of daily life. Only I had tilled a flower and vegetable garden, helped graft fruit trees, cared for baby chicks, and flown down mountains on old wooden skis. This juxtaposition of place had made me as much of the country as of the city. My uncles and aunts in Pennsylvania always introduced me as "the city girl who loves the country." When I was in New York I felt a crushing sense of claustrophobia. We lived in three small rooms and, like many of my friends in the building, I slept in the living room on a "convertible sofa." In Pennsylvania, by contrast, my cousins and I roamed the small hills of the Allegheny Mountains all day. To me this appeared as infinite space abundant with berries and in some places even sweet spring water. Nature represented freedom, and it still does.

Yet in Pennsylvania I also learned a great deal about the suffocating effects of small-town rural America—attitudes, formal education (and the lack of it), what people knew, and what they did not know. New Yorkers were quick and engaged in what was happening in the world. Those in Hastings focused on the small space of the town. They surely were not as well educated or as savvy about a larger world as my family in New York. But they were extremely smart about the natural world.

Although it offered the physical space I missed when I was in New York, Hastings also represented the claustrophobia of provinciality. In the city we went to museums, movies, theater, libraries, ball games. As small as the Brooklyn neighborhood could seem, there was always Manhattan, and it was vast and rich with cultural life, more than I could ever absorb. In Pennsylvania, nature was our entertainment. I loved it, but I would not have wanted to live there all year long. But every year, I counted the days until the summer came and it was time for our return to Hastings, when I would see all my cousins and would be free to wander in the landscape once again.

In both places, life for our relatives was tough. In New York my parents, aunts, and uncles rode the subway to work each morning, suffered the cold and the summer heat. The strain was visible. Many lived in the same building where I grew up in cramped apartments with their families, and all of them worked long hours. But I also came to know what it meant to work hard manual labor on a farm, never being able to leave the animals, trapped by the climate, the crops, and of course the closing of the mines. I saw the poverty of many of my Polish relatives close up. They didn't recognize their lives as impoverished, since most lived at the same level, although some were even poorer.

For most of my childhood, my father ran the auction room on the boardwalk in Point Pleasant, New Jersey, during the summer months while we were in Pennsylvania. After my grandmother died, my mother and I began to spend more time there with him at the Jersey Shore. Then finally I met his friends. They were fast-talking, quick in all ways. They could never have run a farm, fixed a tractor, planted corn, or milked a cow, but they could make a go of it in New York or in New Jersey. Like my Polish relatives in Hastings, they knew how to live on little and still have fun.

These two locations, in their categorical differences and also in their implicit relationship to each other, which I have only come to understand as an adult, have truly formed the way in which I organically gravitate to situations of difference. My movement between them also made me acutely aware of the nuanced way in which social history, religion, class, and ethnicity configure to create the unique experience of place.

As I reconstruct these sites to understand their importance for my life, I need to deploy memory and history. But these two systems of thought, although not antithetical, are in constant tension with each other and in need of negotiation. Memory, as we know, makes no attempt to be objective. It is what one has recorded through the experiential, and it lives in the body within emotional structures that take the shape of stories, narratives, and images. When one tries to contextualize one's deepest memories outside the self, to understand the backdrop for these impressions, then one has to move into the realm of history, where one can accumulate information and historical data that might provide a structure within which to frame the overly heated perceptions of memory. But in fact when memory is truly intense, historical recontextualization can actually increase its power, creating a greater abundance of images within which to place those that already haunt the mind. History may just deepen, broaden, and make more vivid those images memory has already highlighted. Navigating both memory and history, I have tried to create a space within which to honestly reconstruct my relationship to these defining places.

Crown Heights I: The 1950s

Crown Heights, like so much of Brooklyn, is composed of small apartment buildings and one-family dwellings, very densely placed in relationship to one another. It is a particularly good location because from there one can walk to Prospect Park, the Brooklyn Museum, the Brooklyn Botanical Gardens, and the Grand Army Plaza Library. When I was growing up, it was a predominantly Jewish neighborhood in racial and ethnic transition with working-class, middle-class, and upper-middle-class residents living side by side. There had always also been Italians and, in the 1950s, a growing number of African Americans, as well as increasing members of the religious sect of Lubavitcher Jews.

When my father's Russian-born family first came to "the America" (as they always referred to the legend that was the United States), they settled

9

in Williamsburg, Brooklyn, just across that bridge from Manhattan. But by the time I was a child in the 1950s they already had moved to Crown Heights. My grandparents were Orthodox Jews who kept a strict kosher home. My grandfather spent as much time as he could in the synagogue, but he was not a Hasidic Jew. And, like other first-generation Jews born in America, none of his children followed his dedication to religious observance. In fact, when I was a child, the neighborhood comprised many nonobservant Jews like my father and his siblings who, although self-defined as Jewish, were neither invested in rituals nor in the teachings of the Torah. Of all my Jewish cousins, I was the only one interested in studying Hebrew. Although my grandfather would have preferred to teach a grandson, he agreed to work with me. Once a week I would go to his apartment (my beloved grandmother had already died), and we would study Hebrew.

This general lack of religious interest in many of the first- and second-generation Jews in Crown Heights explains why the Lubavitchers, with their extreme religious devotion, appeared so at odds with the rest of the Jewish community at that time. By the early 1960s the balance shifted, however, as the Lubavitcher movement grew dramatically and took over a good deal of the real estate of Crown Heights, and the more secular Jews fled.

Crown Heights has been home to Jews and, in particular, to the Lubavitcher sect of Hasidic Jews since the 1940s, when the sixth Lubavitcher Rebbe, the leader of the sect (who died in 1950), escaped on the eve of the Holocaust and set up a base for his community in Brooklyn. This sect, which has become so omnipresent in Crown Heights, is named after Lubavitch, a town in Belorussia, White Russia, where it originated, a place that was the "center of life for four generations of Chabad Rebbes from the time of Napoleon until the First World War."[2] The Lubavitcher movement is known as *Chabad,* an acronym that in Hebrew designates wisdom, understanding, and knowledge. They are part of a particular lineage of rabbinic philosophy that emphasizes spirituality and emotion. They have a chosen leader, the Rebbe, whom they follow with absolute devotion, although he is a "guide" rather than a "miracle worker." They do not engage with the secular world and, unlike other Jews, they proselytize to bring "secular Jewry" or "nonobservant Jews" into the "Orthodox fold."[3] Their numbers probably never would have grown so large had not so many Jews been killed in the Holocaust and in earlier violent attacks in Russia, thus reducing the numbers of those following other sects and teachings.

After he succeeded his deceased father-in-law as Rebbe in 1950, Rabbi Menachem Mendel Schneerson became increasingly well known. He grew the Lubavitch movement in Brooklyn until, by the 1990s, the community in Crown Heights had become the largest concentration of Lubavitchers in the world. In 1994 there were 300,000 residents in Crown Heights, 80 percent of whom were black, 10 percent of whom were white; most of the latter were Lubavitchers. And since the Rebbe's death in 1994, his house, located at number 770 on the wide boulevard of Eastern Parkway, has become a famous address, "the heart" of the Lubavitcher "court"[4]—a shrine, a site of pilgrimage, and a focal point for this religious movement. For the first time within a self-defined Messianic tradition, and to the horror of other Hasidic sects, as well as to some Lubavitchers themselves, a living Rebbe became equated with the Messiah. Since his death, another Rebbe has not been named, and to this day there are some Lubavitchers who await Rebbe Schneerson's return.

During my childhood, there seemed to be a real antagonism between the nonobservant Jews with whom I grew up and the very ritualized Lubavitchers. To all of us, the presence of these Jews seemed very Other—their clothes, the Yeshivas they established for their children's education, the young people who seemed like old people dressed as their parents—boys in black suits, white shirts and fedoras, or long black coats and wide-brimmed flat black felt hats; young girls in ankle-length drab skirts and hair pulled back who were always coming and going in yellow buses to their own religious schools; and the married women with shaved heads wearing ill-fitting wigs with many young children in tow. To us, these modes of dress and custom seemed extremely outdated. The unfortunate effect of these differences was that we, the Orthodox and Reformed Jews, did not talk to these Hasids, and generally they did not talk to us.

From time to time, however, we did speak to the Lubavitcher boys. We helped them get cigarettes and even sold them cigarette butts from our parents' ashtrays. Although this was nothing to be proud of, it was the only contact we had, and it was exploitative at best. For the most part our worlds were completely isolated, and we were largely invisible to each other. When I was growing up, if you owned a house and you disliked your neighbor, you might sell your house to an African American or to a Lubavitcher—both choices that would likely anger your neighbor since these groups were mistrusted by the other Jews and Italians who lived in Crown Heights at the time. The more secular Jews' discomfort was probably because the Lubavitchers seemed reminiscent of Jews from the Eastern European ghettos, a world with which most Jews attempting to assimilate into U.S. society did not want to identify. The Lubavitchers flaunted their Jewishness and, unfortunately, also their sense of superiority—both behaviors that many Jews in post–World War II America would find troubling.

Another source of the mutual distrust was that since the more secular Jews were so much less observant than they were, the Lubavitchers did not relate to us as Jews. This was particularly painful for those who had survived the Holocaust. There were several such survivors living in my apartment building—my best friend's parents, for example, who themselves had survived the camps but had lost everyone and everything else during the war. This aspect of the neighborhood—the number of refugees (as they were known) living among us who had been in concentration camps—had a profound effect on me. These people had been to hell and back and had numbers tattooed on their arms to prove it. Yet they had survived. Some remarkably went about their daily lives trying to pretend that nothing had happened, while others would not leave their apartments, fearful and paranoid about everyone. Either way, the darkness of their pasts permeated everything. As children we never could really understand what the Holocaust meant, other than that whole families were lost. Some children had no aunts, uncles, or cousins, and on holidays no one visited them and they had nowhere to go. There were no photos of relatives, no mementos. And the past was something no one dared to discuss. Those who had been killed were represented solely by the *Yahrzeit* candles that were lit on Yom Kippur and other holidays on their behalf. Family kitchen counters glowed with light in honor of these innumerable lost souls. For these families to be treated as if they were not Jewish, or not good enough Jews, was extremely painful.

While in the late 1950s this standoff was occurring between Lubavitchers and more secular Jews, tensions were growing with the African-American population. Although I don't recall any direct physical confrontations, I do remember that a group of Lubavitcher men rode around in rattly, big old station wagons patrolling the streets with sticks, brooms, and bats. I realize now that they were a motley crew of vigilantes who called themselves the Maccabees, after "A family of heroes, deliverers of Judea during the Syrian persecution 175–164 B.C."[5] At times they apprehended petty criminals or gang members and beat them up. Later in the 1980s these actions were directed solely at black youth.

On Friday nights the small synagogues that the Lubavitchers had created in the houses they had bought from the nonobservant Jews and Italians came alive with singing and dancing. And on Saturday during the day, Crown Heights looked as I always imagined Jerusalem might on a busy Sabbath afternoon: men in black tunics and black hats, some higher up in the order with big fur hats, even in summer, all walking the streets to the synagogue carrying prayer books.

In the past decade, as Manhattan has become prohibitively expensive, Brooklyn has seen a renaissance, and artists and other young professionals have begun to move into Crown Heights. Although over time this will change the look and feel of the neighborhood, the transformation might not be considerable. The Hasidim will probably always outnumber the artists and every other population. And, as the mecca of the Lubavitcher sect with the greatest educational, spiritual, and commercial infrastructures to accommodate such a religious life, this neighborhood will continue to attract this population from all over the world.

Crown Heights II: The Riots

Brooklyn became the chosen location for many fundamentalist religious groups and extremist cells, in part because it was always an easy destination for those immigrating to America through the entry port of New York. Architecturally, the small affordable apartment buildings form neighborhoods that appear more like a series of connected villages than a great urban center. In spite of all the ethnic rivalries that have existed over the years and the few that have become seriously disruptive and even violent, relationships between working families of different ethnicities were generally positive historically.

Forty years before the 1991 riots in Crown Heights, definite tensions existed between Jews like those in my extended family and newly arriving African Americans. An increase in both the African-American and Puerto Rican populations was occurring all over Brooklyn, and would eventually result in what became known as "white flight" in the late 1950s, when Jews and other whites, frightened by the new racial mix, headed for Long Island ("the island") and other suburbs. It would never have occurred to my parents to move out of the city, but we did relocate to East Flatbush, deeper into Brooklyn, right before I began high school. At that time the East Flatbush neighborhood was predominantly Jewish and Italian. Today it is a mix of Indian, Pakistani, Syrian, Israeli, Palestinian, and Egyptian people—the natural evolution of Brooklyn, a borough whose ethnic groups are constantly in flux.

The move to East Flatbush was to prevent my having to attend Wingate High School, which was becoming predominantly black (although I didn't really understand the import of all this at the time). By the early 1960s there wasn't much of a territorial struggle between Jews and blacks in Crown Heights. The more secular Jews had already left or were leaving. As a child I heard racial slurs from my family and other whites about our black neighbors, but in truth this didn't impact my sense of things greatly because class trumped race in my perception, and in economic terms we all seemed equal to me. When I was in fifth grade my first boyfriend was black. His parents were teachers, and they lived in or owned a beautiful brownstone around the corner from us on President Street. Since space is everything in New York, and was so even then, his family seemed in every way wealthier and more sophisticated than my own. I loved to spend time at his house, and I don't remember any stated objections to this relationship from my family or from his.

But while the Lubavitcher movement grew in Crown Heights through the 1950s, 1960s, and 1970s, so also grew the African-American and West Indian populations. As one can imagine, these cultures had little in common but shared densely populated areas of apartment buildings, small private homes, large private homes, and retail shops. African Americans and West Indians came to feel that the Lubavitchers had been granted special privileges by the local police out of respect for their religious observances and because of their real or imagined political clout. And Lubavitchers became dismayed by the somewhat raucous West Indian parade and by crimes committed by blacks against whites. In 1991 these and other tensions exploded.

For most New Yorkers and non–New Yorkers, Crown Heights first came into their consciousness when the 1991 riots erupted. But what happened in Crown Heights in August 1991 was not a surprise to anyone who was familiar with this neighborhood. It seemed like the inevitable outcome of the tensions that had begun when I was a child. The incident is important for what it tells us about race in America—the fragile balance of multiple diverse communities often trying to share limited space. The narrative that follows has been culled from several sources, including Edward S. Shapiro's book, *Crown Heights: Blacks, Jews, and the 1991 Brooklyn Riot.*[6]

On the day the incident occurred, Rebbe Schneerson was returning from the Montefiore Cemetery in Queens where he went each week to pray at the graves of his wife and father-in-law. He would often spend several hours reading aloud from the numerous letters he had received that week from his followers all over the world, asking his father-in-law for specific guidance on secular and religious matters. This meditation to receive answers for his followers is a contemplative tradition of rabbis brought from Russia. Schneerson was returning with his motorcade from one of these expeditions on August 19, 1991, at nightfall when a terrible accident took place.

Because there had been threats against his life by other Orthodox sects some years before, he had been promised and given a police escort whenever he left the neighborhood. This protection itself was a source of tension among other constituencies of Crown Heights. This night the convoy included several cars and a station wagon with four Lubavitchers that remained behind the Rebbe's car to keep it from being rear-ended. The station wagon lagged behind the other cars as the convoy crossed the intersection of Utica Avenue and President Street in the heart of Crown Heights. It is not clear in the reports whether the driver of the station wagon was driving too quickly, perhaps to catch up with the Rebbe's car, but he did go through at least one yellow light and maybe even a red light. The station wagon hit a car going through an intersection, then, careening out of control, leapt up onto the sidewalk and ran over a seven-year-old Guyanese boy named Gavin Cato and his cousin Angela Cato, also seven years old, pinning the boy beneath the car. Gavin Cato arrived at the hospital already dead from the impact. His cousin Angela survived with multiple fractures.

It was determined immediately that the driver was not intoxicated and that what had occurred was definitely an accident. Although the driver of the station wagon might have been driving too quickly to catch up with the Rebbe's caravan, he was not convicted of involuntary manslaughter in Gavin Cato's death.

Immediately after the accident took place, the four men driving the station wagon were pulled from the car and beaten by African Americans who witnessed the collision. Rumors were flying, and some on the scene believed that Cato's death could have been prevented if the Jewish-owned ambulance that came to the scene for the beaten driver would also have taken the young boy to the hospital. There were others who thought that Cato might have survived if his father had been allowed to remove his body from under the car. These speculations and others fueled an already intense situation. Thus began the most violent and extensive anti-Semitic incident that has ever occurred in Brooklyn.

The riot's first victim was Yankel Rosenbaum, a visiting Hasidic scholar from Australia, not a Lubavitcher, who just happened to be walking in Crown Heights a few hours after the accident. A group of young African-American men surrounded him, shouting something like, "Let's get the Jew." One of the attackers fatally stabbed him seven times. Crown Heights then truly erupted, and the riots that ensued went on for four days. Factions developed among the West Indian, Trinidadian, Guyanese, and African-American populations. Leaders like Al Sharpton took up the cause and conflated these culturally unique groups, identifying them all as black—although not all agreed to this designation. Some turned against Mayor David Dinkins—the first African-American mayor of New York—and his desire for "integration and reconciliation." Surprisingly and unfortunately, while all this was going on, the Rebbe, previously outspoken and very public in his role as leader of the Lubavitchers, remained silent. As a result of these riots, the neighborhood gained its national reputation as a site of conflict, and relations between Jews and other ethnic groups in the neighborhood have remained strained to this day.

When Jack and I pulled up to Carroll Street, just north of where I grew up, on that afternoon a year and some months after the 1991 riots, it is not surprising that there were still police patrols and that the neighborhood, for the first time, felt to me like a true ghetto, or a gated community, where an outsider could be spotted, interrogated, and evaluated as someone who should or should not be allowed to walk the streets, someone who might or might not be capable of aggravating existent tensions.

The *Mischling*

While living in Crown Heights as a child, I don't recall having any behaviors directed at my friends or me that one could call anti-Semitic. Although there were tensions between different Jewish groups and an overbearing memory of past crimes against Jews, all of which I have described, we did not experience overt anti-Semitism. But when my gentile mother married my Jewish father in 1938, after many years of deliberation, it was a very serious event. It was as if they had married across race.

Although I did not know anyone else who was of mixed religion when I was growing up, nor did I ever think of myself as mixed race at the time, there were countless jokes in the culture about Jewish men marrying non-Jewish women, to their families' horror. Here's an archetypal one: "With great trepidation a Jewish son tells his mother, 'Ma, I want to marry a non-Jewish girl, a *shiksa*.' He waits for her response. When it is not offered, he asks, 'Mom, are you upset?' 'Oh, no dear,' replies the mother, who then starts to leave the room. 'Mom, where are you going?' asks the distraught son. The mother replies, 'Oh, just out to the kitchen to stick my head in the oven.'"

There was lots of talk about how "special" my mother was, and in fact she was very loved by my father's family. Somehow she broke through whatever stereotypes they had about non-Jewish women. But, as a child of this mix, this miscegenation, I was considered a complex entity. And it is only now, as an adult, that I truly understand the weight of its meaning historically.

In Sander Gilman's text, *Franz Kafka, the Jewish Patient,* he describes how in Prague at the turn of the century this notion of a crossbreed half-Jew— *the mischling*—was a very potent image. He quotes a German text from 1912: "The children of such marriages (between Jews and non-Jews) ... even though they are so very beautiful and so very talented, seem to lack a psychological balance that is provided by pure racial stock. We find all too often intellectually or morally unbalanced individuals, who decay ethically or end in suicide or madness."[7]

This notion of the *mischling* had great meaning for Kafka because he himself felt he was a complex Jew with multiple forces pulling on him and defining him—a German father, an Italian mother, a religion that had been diluted, a culture that was assimilating. *Mischling,* according to Agamben, signified "People with only one Jewish grandparent,"[8] an official German designation as of September 15, 1935, for those who were neither of pure Aryan descent nor of total Jewish descent. The scorn attached to the crossbreed is not something that simply disappeared after the Holocaust. In fact, the fear of mixing races is still alive and well in Brooklyn. As an adult I was shocked to learn that there are still sects of Jews in Brooklyn who not only have an aversion to mixed marriages but who have also formalized their rancor into a powerful set of laws of which they seem quite proud.

Among the Syrian Jewish community in Brooklyn, there is today an "Edict" very much in use. It was developed by Syrian Rabbis in 1935 in Brooklyn, and it makes it quite clear that mixed marriages are serious business that must be punished if the Jewish "race" is to remain pure. The Edict proclaims: "No male or female member of our community has the right to intermarry with non-Jews; this law covers conversion, which we consider to be fictitious and valueless."[9] In 1946, the following text was added: "The rabbi will not perform Religious Ceremonies for such unkosher couples. The Congregation's premises will be banned to them for use of any religious or social nature. . . . After death of said person, he or she is not to be buried on [sic] the Cemetery of our community . . . regardless of financial considerations."[10] The newest version, issued in 2006 and signed by 225 rabbis and lay leaders, is testimony to the growth of the community and the enduring power of the Edict: "Never accept a convert or a child born of a convert. Push them away with strong hands from our community. Why? Because we don't want gentile characteristics."[11]

It is amazing that this type of direct assault on the mixing of races is still articulated without any shame whatsoever. Of all people, Jews should have learned the consequences of such ideals of racial purity. The Edict surely makes clear that the issue of intermarriage is not about religion but about race. If it were truly simply a religious or cultural issue, conversion would be an acceptable solution. But conversion is completely scorned, since anyone of any race or ethnicity could then be considered a Jew. A 2007 article in the *New York Times Magazine* cites several instances of families excommunicating their own children after they intermarried. Once banned from the community, these children were never seen again. Yet those who committed serious white-collar crimes, even against other members of their community, have been forgiven and taken back into the fold. It would seem that for these Syrian Jews, the truly unforgivable act of marrying outside the race is denounced as forcefully by this group as homosexuality. (The designer Isaac Mizrahi was born into this community, but because he is self-identified as gay, he is now considered persona non grata.)[12]

Although the Edict is very extreme, much more extreme than anything I have ever seen or heard from Jews living in America, it lays out a series of concepts about marriage, loyalty, and bloodlines that exist in some form throughout other homogeneous Jewish communities. The *New York Times Magazine* article talks about the need for Syrian Jews to build a fortress around their community, an "iron wall of self-separation," but that this could not be done in "the Hasidic way. . . . Dressing the men in costumes of ancient design, physically segregating women and making sure that children received nothing in the way of useful secular education." This simply would not do. "After all, the Syrian men couldn't be expected to make money if they looked like figures from 18th-century Poland."[13] Of course it must be said that the Hasidim have been financially successful in multiple businesses—diamond trading, for one, and more recently technology—in spite of their dress.

Whether latent or overt, it is not surprising that even between Orthodox and Reformed Jews, being half-Jewish and half-Catholic was very problematic. And although my identity was not presented to me in Crown

Heights as a problem, it was made clear to me by my parents that some day I would have "to choose" my religion. This was because it was assumed that when I would want to marry, my choice of religion would determine whom I *could* marry. Obviously, this was all very abstract to me as a child. What *was* real then was the sense that I had to decide something I did not know how to decide. My parents, loving and wonderful as they were, had no idea how to guide me in this. To this day, whenever I feel unable to make an important or unimportant decision and seem to get stuck halfway, I say to myself, "Oh, I see. This is the 'should I be Catholic or should I be Jewish' dilemma." It still affects me, creating an unconscious anxiety about choosing correctly. But the most disconcerting aspects of my dual-religion experience were made manifest to me in my other, very different home in rural Pennsylvania.

Hastings

When my maternal grandmother was still alive and whenever we had an opportunity, my mother and I would leave my father in Brooklyn, working, and we would board a train at Penn Station and head for Altoona, Pennsylvania, the closest destination to my mother's family home. In Hastings, men were farmers, coal miners, or both. My extended family—uncles, aunts, and cousins—could fix or build anything. My mother used to say that when she was a child the only things they bought were shoes. Everything else they made by hand, grew in the fields, picked in the wild, or hunted in the forest.

When in Hastings we stayed with my aunts and cousins in my grandmother's house. It was a two-storied wood-frame house covered with brown ceramic tiles. It had several bedrooms, a large lilac tree right next to the coal bin, a front porch swing at each level, a well, a pump, an outhouse, a coal stove, grates and dampers on the floors, and a trap door between the first and second floors that was closed at night to retain the heat. Given the small, uninsulated houses of the mining settlements in which my grandmother must have lived when she first came from Poland, my grandmother must have found this house that my uncles built for her quite luxurious. She planted a beautiful flower garden around it, and it was in her bed, in that very house, that she died. The house was about two miles from the center of a town that, even in the 1950s, was like a small ecosystem that still revolved around coal.

The history of coal mining in Pennsylvania runs parallel to the Industrial Revolution and the development of the United States as a world power.[14] Poles were easily lured to America in the mid- to late 1880s because of dire economic conditions in Poland. That first wave of immigrants came mostly from rural economies without a great deal of industrial experience. Pennsylvania offered opportunity. It had already become a great industrial state

Resting with the load at the head of the slope. Shaft #6 Pennsylvania Coal Co, 1911.
Photograph by Lewis Wickes Hine. Library of Congress Prints and Photographs Division Washington, D.C.

based on textile, iron, and glass works. There was land to be farmed and money to be made.

The War of 1812 cut the colonies off from supplies from England and even from Virginia coal. The country had to become more independent and resourceful. New forms of fuel had to be developed, and manufacturers who wanted to succeed needed to move away from wood-derived charcoal, which was responsible for rapidly depleting the forests and had also become quite expensive. Once coal was discovered (and rumor has it this happened when a trapper made a campfire against a small mountain and set the hill on fire), it became the solution. Anthracite coal was a resource Pennsylvania could offer to the rest of the country. And once Pittsburgh was able to run steam engines more cheaply than England, there was a revolution in iron making and an increasing independence from foreign sources that further propelled the American Industrial Revolution. As a result, among other groups, 2.5 million Poles were lured to America from 1850 to 1914 to work.

This is the period when my grandfather first arrived, followed by my grandmother and her two first-born children. At this time there was simultaneously a great exodus of people attempting to avoid military service in Germany, Austria-Hungary, and Russia. And there were also those leaving Eastern Europe because of religious, cultural, and political oppression. Most of the Poles who left came to Pennsylvania for land and for jobs. The town was incorporated by enterprising coal men:

19

In 1887 Governor Beaver, General Hastings and Colonel Spangler, all of Belle-fonte, and Robert Coleman of Lebanon incorporated under the title of Blubaker Coal company and bought some 14,000 acres of coal lands in Elder, Susquehanna, Barr and Caroll Townships. It was intended that the company be named Brubaker, the name of the creek ... that flows through the present town of Hastings.... The name Blubaker was the result of an error in printing.... The first car of coal was shipped from Hastings in July 1888 by the Chest Creek Coal and Coke company. The town was laid out in 1888.[15]

By 1950 the population of Hastings was 1,846. It was a small town, and my family knew and was related to a great many of its residents. We would have attended the baptism parties, the weddings, and the feast days together. For most of my childhood years, the mines were still in opera-tion. The production levels had declined, especially in relationship to the demand for coal during World War II, when the need was so great that miners were offered military deferments. But by the 1950s other forms of fuel were beginning to take the place of coal, and many of the mines were cutting back or closing. Even so, the effects of decades of mining were still apparent everywhere.

In the summers we swam in a dam that we reconstructed each year out of sod, but the water was orange, filled with sulfuric runoffs from the mines. There are 350 miles of streams in western Pennsylvania that are still tainted by this pollution. Before 1977, mines were just abandoned, the doors to the shafts simply boarded up without consequence to the owners. No one took responsibility for cleaning up the sites or reversing any of the negative effects to the environment. There were "bony piles," as we called them, everywhere. In Maryland these slag heaps could be a quarter of a mile long and fifty feet tall. In Hastings they were like small hills composed of pieces of porous rock that were the residues, the throw-away piles of ore that were not pure coal. There were nights when they would ignite and glow green and blue. These are now also referred to as "gob piles." In areas where the mining was for bituminous coal, the process was different, but the environmental effects were the same. The word "gob" is short for "garbage of bituminous." In these areas the piles are tar-colored waste heaps made of shale and iron pyrite mixed with coal. Iron pyrite is fool's gold, and when it is exposed to water and oxygen it can create sulfuric acid. When it rains these piles leach out a black sludge that is a dangerous mix of chemicals, and when the rain dries up, bits of dust fly off from these dumps, covering everything around them with toxic dust.

We didn't know any of this was toxic at the time. We played on these hills, ran and slid down them, got cut up and bruised by them. But no one seemed to know to avoid them or to keep us out of the orange creek. The result was that later, much later, the rate of cancer became very high (and this toxicity in the water and the soil does make me wonder about my grandmother's death from uterine cancer in the 1950s). This situation, combined with the presence of black lung disease, has made the aged population quite unhealthy.

In the 1950s, the miners returning from work stopped at my grandmother's saloon, which my uncles had built for her and my aunts to run as a way of earning money when they went off to the war. The miners came in covered in coal dust. They drank shots and beer—boilermakers—and my aunts and my mother worked the tavern. It was a social place, a beer hall as well, where weddings, christenings, and other parties were held.

When I was a child, only my Uncle Jakie was still left working the mines. We often brought him his lunch. But when the mines began to shut down in the late 1950s and the town's residents became desperate, all my uncles had to leave for the big cities to find work—to Cleveland and the auto industry, to Chicago and the stockyards, or to New York for myriad small industrial possibilities.

What the apartment building in Crown Heights was to the Jewish family, my grandmother's house was to the Catholic family. We all convened there in the summer to be with my grandmother. My Aunt Helen and my cousins stayed in Hastings to care for her. For the most part, that world was a matriarchy of women and children while the men remained in the cities to work. My father flew into Altoona a few times during the summer. Definitely not a country guy, he often was lulled to sleep by the silence of nature. I would now guess that he must have been exhausted, working hard in the summer heat of New York—pre–air-conditioning—and then coming home to a hot, lonely apartment, trying to make a buck and missing us.

Although there was a very strong sense of family connectedness and solidarity in Hastings, it was there that I became painfully aware that I was Other to my Polish-Catholic cousins. When we were young, they liked to remind me that because my father was Jewish, no matter what I did I would never see Jesus as they were able to do. I'd never have his blessing, and my mother and I would both surely "burn in hell." It was so shocking and so humiliating to me at the time that I don't remember ever daring to discuss this with anyone. The beds that we slept on each had a crucifix hanging above, a reminder of how different this home was from my life in New York and how difficult it was in this environment to counter the certainty of my Catholic cousins that my mother and I were damned.

Since then I have learned that this type of attitude about Jews came from a very deep and old prejudice among Polish Catholics. It is what Zygmunt Bauman calls "fossilized anti-Semitism."[16] "The most spectacular of Holocaust survivals.... It now lives, so to speak, without its traditional environment; it is truly out of its element."[17] It is the anti-Semitism of the post-war trauma kept alive in the so-called New World by those for whom Catholicism was the only imaginable religion. (One of my cousins became a priest.) But this anti-Semitism was significant for me since it joined the two places of my childhood historically, although I didn't understand that at the time.

The racism of Poland to the Jews about which Bauman writes so eloquently in his essay, "Assimilation into Exile: The Jew as a Polish Writer," articulates this connection to Europe in a way that was unimaginable to me when I was growing up. These cultures were disconnected in America. No one talked to me about what had happened in Poland or the source of my cousin's misplaced attitudes. World War II and its aftermath were very visible to me in New York—the refugees, the camp survivors, a sense of a horrific past, were around me daily—but Pennsylvania seemed to be all about starting over and believing in a hopeful future.

Bauman, himself a Pole, has written eloquently about the guilt felt by Poles for what occurred during the war and how their racism was even more virulent *after* the war. Jews who survived returned to Poland only to find their homes and businesses taken over by Poles. In Isaac Deutscher's terms, cited by Bauman, the Polish Gentile "*lumpenproletariat* was turned into the *lumpenbourgeoisie*" overnight.[18] For Bauman, the Poles' guilt for abuses toward Jews runs very deep and has been masked by an even more profound racist attitude. He writes, "The stubborn fact cannot be washed away: a great nation, which for eight hundred years shared the glory and the misery of Polish history, was rounded up and murdered and its death was not prevented. This means guilt."[19]

Topographies

Although the fragment of Polish history just described was unknown to me as a child, it now helps me to understand to what degree these childhood incidents influenced where my religious and cultural affinities finally came to rest. I also now see clearly that the experience of my Polish-Catholic family transported to rural America was much closer to that of my Russian-Jewish family, transported to the Brooklyn ghetto, than I ever would have guessed. These ethnic populations that seemed so completely disparate to me as a child had actually existed in close proximity geographically and historically before arriving in America and had brought that reality with them to their new lives.

I have held these two locations in my head and in my heart for my entire life. They were both home—places I loved filled with people I loved. They were also the sites of grave alienation, as I tried at that time so soon after the war, in both locations, to embody the complexity of my own duality. And, as is often the case in the lives of children, my realities and complexities came first. I did not understand the treacherous navigation my parents must have had to perform to find their balance. Like all children, swathed in their own narcissism, I knew only what anchored or unanchored me.

What did my mother feel in relationship to her Otherness, both to the Jews of Crown Heights—my father's family—and to her own Polish family? What pain did my father experience when he thought his family's prejudice might hurt my mother? Or me? From where did my parents gather the courage to simply go beyond all of this and form such a profoundly loving union? This is terrain I can only now imagine, since I never explored it with them while they were alive.

So much of what I think of as home is now just memory. These locations are fixed in time, and as I read, study, and imagine what the actual context of these situations might have been, that historical time that one can create around these internal events becomes, at best, a parallel universe that never really affects or intersects with those memories of childhood that run before me as a movie repeating itself on a loop. I can understand the contextualization for them all, but my version is made of different stuff than the verifiable or the historical fact. It is formed out of the imagination—that amalgam of memory and embellishment that lives primarily in the senses. All of it can be brought back by images, colors, smells, tastes, the texture of the air. As Proust has chronicled for all eternity, anything of the senses can be the *Petite Madeleine* that tumbles us back into something that is completely unique to our own experience and whose dimensionality only film, literature, or art can truly begin to represent. Nobel Laureate Orhan Pamuk writes, "This world that I had created like a man digging a well with a needle would then seem truer than all else."[20]

Several years ago, before I decided to buy an apartment in Brooklyn in 2000, to reinhabit that zone of ancestors and memory, I made another trip to Crown Heights with an artist friend, Susanna Coffey. I had left Brooklyn long ago but had driven by the neighborhood probably once a year for all those years. And when I did, I was always struck by how little the look of it had changed. Sometimes I would stop the car and simply observe, but this expedition with Susanna in the late 1990s was the first in a long while when I actually chose to walk around.

In those days Susanna was driving a big pickup truck, and we parked it on the street in front of the apartment building where I grew up, 424 Albany Avenue, right across from what was once the Peck Memorial Hospital. It was spring, and the streets were crowded with Lubavitcher men, women, and children. When I stepped out of the car, I had the unique sensation that I was floating, not really connecting with the ground, but, rather, was just being propelled forward, in the body but out of the body. I was levitating, or so it seemed. A young Lubavitcher woman pushing a baby carriage approached us immediately. "Are you new to the neighborhood?" she asked. "No, I'm actually old to the neighborhood," I responded, "And it's old to me. I used to live right here," and I gestured behind me to the apartment of my childhood. "Well then," she said, "Are you Jewish?" Too long a story, I thought, so

I said, "Yes," lying and knowing full well that for this Lubavitcher woman, the fact of my Catholic mother made me absolutely a non-Jew. Then to Susanna, who had long blond hair and was wearing it down, she asked, "Are you Jewish?" Susanna shook her head no. She then handed each of us a flyer. Mine said, "Remember the Rebbe," and she pointed to a banner that crossed the entirety of Montgomery Street. It read: "The Rebbe Is Coming. The Rebbe is coming." Susanna's flyer was less promising: "Those who do not practice the way of the Torah are fornicators, alcoholics, sinners." "Guaranteed to convert me," said Susanna to the woman, who then walked away.

It was at this point that the floating became acute, and what I thought at the time was this: *All of it is dreaming itself, and I alone am not in the dream. It is not my dream they are dreaming, yet I too am here with them.* Is this what happens when consciousness meets the unconscious while awake? Or is this what happens when memory confronts history and cannot be reconciled?

We walked the streets as if we belonged, mingling with the Hasidim, and Susanna saw a young girl in a blue flared coat and patent leather shoes skipping in front of us. "That's you when you were small," she said. "You are walking behind yourself. Can you remember what you were like?" We were both captured in another universe, not of now, not of then, but of the then in the now. I was home, but it was home as it has lived inside the imagination and the unconscious for decades—now externalized and manifested in the present.

This is the stuff that one struggles to re-create in writing and in art. It is the experience one desperately wants to communicate to others. But in this otherworldly instance, the effect was not so much to be reflected on, but simply to be lived.

Although I have not returned to Hastings, I know that it has truly changed and has become a sad place. There is no industry now except health care institutions providing treatment for the retired mine workers and others who live on pensions, compensation, or black lung disability. The highways have cut through the center of the town, making it easier to go east and west but splitting the town into fragments. The family home was sold long ago when my mother's eldest brother, my Uncle Lou, who had inherited the property, died. I still need to return, a trip I had intended to take with my mother. Now I will have to go alone.

A Form of Return

Crown Heights and Hastings were the defining places; they haunt me and strengthen me still. To go back to them through the speculative act of writing is an attempt to reinhabit them as a home of my own making.

As Hannah Arendt wrote in a letter to Karl Jaspers in 1946, when she was already living in New York, "Writing [is a] form of return." To send an essay to Germany to be published in a journal right after the war (as per his request) would be like going home, she speculated. In her mind a Jew could not return after the war "as if nothing had happened."[21] Nor could one send a piece of writing as if it were disconnected from the self. To Arendt, one could only write—that is, return home—as a Jew. So if she were to write for Jaspers's journal (i.e., if she were to return), then she had to do so as a Jew writing about the situation of Jews. Nothing less would have been acceptable.

I am grateful to have attempted my own return to these originary places in writing and to have begun a process of navigation—from there (memory) to here (the present). But the *here* in which I have landed is finally not a physical, geographical, or even temporal place. Rather, it is a virtual space of ideas, a familiar place of emotions and situations made of the stories and images that I have replayed throughout my life. Here they are given a foundation in historical fact, a new heft and solidity that buoys them up. Writing in this way has given me a new way to tell the story, not just to the reader but also to myself and, in the telling, to have created a place within which to imagine the momentary integration of the parts—in other words, a new narrative.

The comings and goings of my childhood, physical and cultural, surely made a traveler of me, and thus I have repeatedly sought to experience the uniqueness of place in Europe, Asia, Africa, and Latin America. But I have also attempted to encounter similar experiences in books, art, language, and culture. For decades I have written about art, artists, and social action as location—places of contemplation where one learns how to understand the world or where one recognizes one's own already existent understanding of the world by seeing it reflected back and deepened in multiples. And I've also written about the experience of location as art. Having thus approached art, space, and even significant historical figures as sites of trauma and investigation, I was heartened to encounter my favorite philosophical geographer Yi-Fu Tuan talking about location in similarly unorthodox ways: "The arts too can be a home. Or make us feel more at home. Yet even more than geographical place, they have the power to disturb or exalt, and so, like the great teachings of religion, remind us that we are fundamentally homeless."[22]

For Yi-Fu Tuan,

> Place—geographical place—is a material environment. It can be natural, as, for example an unspoiled forest or seashore and it can be—to varying degrees— artifactual, everything from a thatched hut to a glass-and-steel high rise. In the process of considering place as an architectural artwork, we may be led to ask whether other artworks such as a painting, photograph, poem, story, movie, dance, or musical composition can also be a place—a virtual place.
>
> Isn't it true that we pause before them, rest in them, and are, in one sense or another, nurtured by them, as we rest and are nurtured by the towns and cities and landscapes we live in or visit?[23]

Yi-Fu Tuan also quotes Bernard Berenson: "A painter's special challenge is to convey, more rapidly and unfailingly than nature would do, the consciousness of an unusually intense degree of well-being."[24]

Surely this sense of "well-being" can be found in paintings like Vermeer's, for example, in which rooms seem to inhabit states of reflection and calm. But such virtual spaces also can become sites of true interrogation that engage the senses, the memory, and society while critically challenging us to find and define the phenomenological world and our place within it. This, of course, is also true of the physical environment, where there are so many sites of terror, tragedy, trauma, and uncertainty. As upsetting as it can be, visiting these places can also help us to structure the way in which we conceptualize, frame, and come to understand the world as we move on and beyond history. There is also little doubt that some of the most innovative thinking takes place between these localities where the boundaries of the physical, conceptual, and philosophical become conterminous.

Therefore, if one is thinking in place and truly engaging each situation, even those of one's own creation—as in writing or art making—there is a requirement that you not only enter into such spaces, move around in them, examine and try to make sense of their interiorities and exteriorities, but that also, miraculously, through a combination of thought and action, you find a way out, knowing that there can be no real resolution to the questions posed, only a process of framing and reframing, which inevitably moves the investigation forward.

In Zygmunt Bauman's discussion of Polish poetry and Jewish assimilation after the war, he quotes Arthur Sandauer, who writes about the Polish-Jewish writer Julian Tuwin. This poet became important to Polish society, not because he successfully assimilated into Polish culture, but because he did not. Nonetheless, he found a home or shelter in the Polish language itself. Sandauer writes of Tuwin, "Essentially, assimilation did not succeed; what succeeded was the poetry, born of that failed assimilation and of unhappy love for Poland. . . . As the other Poland refused to accept him, Polish language [sic] remained his true homeland."[25]

Tuwin and others like him were at home writing in their mother tongue, Polish, about their homelessness—the failed attempts to be accepted by Polish society. That their writing successfully articulated this complexity, then found a place in the national archive, and became part of Polish cultural history is ironic. That it actually helped to define Polishness is absurd. Yet these writers' articulation of Otherness allowed the image of Polishness to solidify as a concept and provided the historical construct that would make Polish national identity possible, although not for them.

Adorno wrote, "For a man who no longer has a homeland, writing becomes a place to live."[26] This can be said of all art making. It provides structures for the representation of contradictions and the articulation of the sense of statelessness. And in so doing it offers a partial, temporal solution for the problem of not belonging by becoming a new locale, an invented one, where even those traditionally positioned on the outside finally find their way in.

Notes

1. Yi-Fu Tuan, *Place, Art, and Self* (Santa Fe, NM: Center for American Places, 2004), 44.

2. Jerome R. Mintz, *Hasidic People: A Place in the New World* (Cambridge, MA: Harvard University Press, New Edition, 1994), 43–59.

3. Ibid.

4. Ibid.

5. *The American College Dictionary*, ed. C. L. Barnhart (New York: Random House, 1963), 729.

6. Edward S. Shapiro, *Crown Heights: Blacks, Jews, and the 1991 Brooklyn Riot* (Waltham, MA: Brandeis University Press, 2006). Another source of information was Jonathan Rieder's essay, "Crown of Thorns: The Roots of the Black-Jewish Feud," *The New Republic*, October 14, 1991, 26–31.

7. Sander Gilman, *Franz Kafka, the Jewish Patient* (New York: Routledge, 1996), 14.

8. Giorgio Agamben, *Remnants of Auschwitz: The Witness and the Archive*, trans. Daniel Heller-Roazan (New York: Zone Books, 1999), 84.

9. Zev Chafets, "The SY Empire: The Syrian Jews of Gravesend Brooklyn," *New York Times Magazine*, October 14, 2007, 84.

10. Ibid.

11. Ibid.

12. Ibid., 87.

13. Ibid., 84.

14. Several sources have been very valuable in helping me to understand the history of coal mining in Pennsylvania, including Thomas Dublin, *When the Mines Closed: Stories of Struggles in Hard Times* (Ithaca, NY: Cornell University Press, 1996), and Barbara Freese, *Coal: A Human Story* (London: Penguin Books, 2004).

15. Hastings, PA. Borough Website, Hastings Settlement, www.hastingsboro.com.

16. Zygmunt Bauman, "Assimilation Into Exile: The Jew as a Polish Writer," in *Exile and Creativity: Signposts, Travelers, Outsiders, Backward Glances*, ed. Susan Rubin Suleiman (Durham, NC: Duke University Press, 1998), 333.

17. Ibid.

18. Ibid.

19. Ibid., 332.

20. Orhan Pamuk, *Other Colors: Essays and a Story* (New York: Knopf, 2007), 414.

21. Hannah Arendt, Letter to Karl Jaspers, January 29, 1946, in *The Portable Hannah Arendt*, ed. Peter Baehr (New York: Penguin, 2003), 25–31.

22. Yi-Fu Tuan, *Place, Art, and Self*, 44.

23. Ibid., 3.

24. Ibid., 21.

25. Bauman, "Assimilation Into Exile," 338.

26. Theodor Adorno, *Minima Moralia,* trans. E. F. N. Jephcott (Frankfurt: Verso, 1974), 87.

2
Museums and the Neutralization of Culture
A Response to Adorno

⊸

Museums are like the family sepulchres of works of art. They testify to the neutralization of culture.[1]

Dreaming in the Dark

As a child, I spent many of my after-school and weekend hours in the Brooklyn Museum. I lived just a few blocks away, and several times a week I walked down Eastern Parkway, stopping before the Botanical Gardens, to enter a quiet, dark, somber lobby that in those days was cluttered with glass cases filled with Egyptian mummies and fabulous African ceremonial objects—hence the low protective lighting.

The mummies in particular made a profound impression on me. And although I cannot reconstruct exactly why that was, I have never forgotten the drawing classes I took at the museum every Saturday for one year. Our assignment was always the same: Sit in front of the mummies and draw. Mine were awful. I couldn't draw. I still can't. In that context, it seemed that either you could or couldn't draw. No one there advised us that you could *learn* to draw—something my years at art schools now have taught me is possible. But even as wretched as my pencil representations of these dried-up treasures were, and as torturous as these exercises then seemed, those swathed, shrunken bodies haunt me still.

After hours spent sitting in the dark, we were free to roam the museum as we chose. I always went upstairs to the "period rooms," which fascinated me. They were life-sized re-creations of traditional sitting rooms and other domestic spaces from England, France, and America. The rooms of the original Dutch settlers of New York, particularly their kitchens, attracted my greatest attention. I was probably intrigued by the fact that New York had once been New Amsterdam and that the Dutch had lived in the same place I now inhabited. I had forgotten this fascination until my first trip to the Netherlands, when I marveled at Amsterdam's similarities to New York; the color of the wood, the shape of the houses, and the look of the city all reminded me of the New York of my childhood and the New Amsterdam of the past that I viewed through these simulacra.

There is no doubt that I loved then what Paul Valery called "the magnificent chaos of the museum."[2] In those days, more than now, objects from all over the world created an all-encompassing internal clutter that filled the space and overwhelmed the senses. Perhaps most significant for me and for my childhood friends was the feel of those galleries—solemn, cavernous, stuffed with things, and mostly empty of people. We claimed this space as ours, an extension of the cinema of our dream lives. In my memory at least, entry was free for children. And although I'm sure there were guards, I don't remember seeing any. Nor do I remember the shops and the selling of objects that are now so ubiquitous. What I *do* remember is the freedom the museum represented. It was our place, albeit a grown-up place, within which we could be transported to multiple other realities and moments of cultural history. It made Brooklyn seem huge. It made my life seem huge. I could roam many continents in an afternoon, surrounded by sacred objects from Africa, India, or Brazil. I could go upstairs to American landscape painting and experience my own continent, one that I had yet to explore. While looking at European painting, I could dream of the rainy streets of Paris and battles raging on the English Channel. I could journey back in history aware of the possibility that I might actually travel forward into such realities in the future. At this time I didn't think about those who made the objects, and I certainly didn't attempt to deconstruct the meaning of my gaze. The most important thing for me, then, was that it was *our* museum to roam in freely, just as we did on our streets.

To this day I attribute the ease, excitement, and awe with which I enter historical museums to the experiences of that time. And as forbidding and pretentious as such spaces can be, I never feel intimidated, having gained my sense of entitlement early on by drawing those mummies. On reflection, it seems quite logical that for decades later I would inhabit a world in which a great historical museum loomed large and that, at times, I would refer to it as "my museum."

I was a true spectator caught in the spectacle—the museum of those early years, a site of play and awe. Today, although I can still become excited by what I find when I enter such encyclopedic museums, my intellect eventually forces me into a criticality about many aspects of the museum world. Apart from observing what constituencies the space serves, I now think about how the objects are arranged, the context they are given—what is allowed in and what is kept out. I reflect upon cultural difference, how that is represented and what is presented as familiar. I question how much we need to know beforehand to understand the work in relationship to how much we are actually given. And although I easily can still get caught up in some fantastic exhibition, at some point I inevitably ask myself these questions: What is the intention of the institution? What is it trying to achieve? Whose interests does it serve? Whose interests does it *pretend* to serve?

Flow

The Art Institute of Chicago sits at the heart of the city and, like the Field Museum of Natural History, occupies a central place in the collective imagination of Chicago. It competes with no other institution for cultural weight or *gravitas*, breadth, and depth. No matter how cutting-edge or established a museum of contemporary art may become, it can never achieve such resonance. No matter how great a natural history museum may be, and the Field Museum certainly is at the top of this list, it does not have the romance of a historical art museum. And although contemporary art museums can exhibit very significant work, in practice they cannot assume to take a stand on what needs to be remembered, studied, archived, and preserved for all major civilizations. This is the mission of a historical museum that is a repository of culture, or of that which has been determined by the art historical and curatorial world to be culture.

And because I used to move within the structures of this world as represented by the Art Institute of Chicago many days of the week, I have also had unique opportunities to observe closely its topography, flow patterns, and geography. Such a museum moves glacially, the great entrance hall its terminal moraine. Speed is antithetical to its mission. If anything, institutions such as the Art Institute seek to slow the world down.

Museums need to be secure. They house objects for safekeeping, and so the works are generally protected from theft, the elements, and the overthrow of governments. They are reposited or repositioned in a timeless zone where, in many museums, they will stay in the same spot for the duration of our lives. We locate them there in our own memories, not where they were created and not necessarily in the space for which they were intended, but there, in the space where we first saw them. When I heard of the theft of two Van Gogh paintings from the Van Gogh Museum in Amsterdam several years ago, I was horrified. One assumes that these treasures will be safe in their customary place on the wall forever. That stability is part of what is expected of museums. And when objects are loaned to other institutions, it is surprising to find their original location empty, often replaced by a small printed sign or a small reproduction of the work. One connotation of a repository is "a burial vault."[3] For the most part, when we as viewers are not concentrating on a piece in the collection, in effect it is dead, unanimated to us. When we engage the objects, or when they are repositioned in a special focused exhibition, they come alive.

We assume that the objects stored in such a sepulchral space will be stable spatially and temporally. As Marc Augé says about monuments, they seem to us as "above temporal contingencies," and they "thus enable people to think in terms of continuity through the generations."[4] Museums have always been understood as presenting historical and cultural evolutions. One can drop in to see a special show, a sculpture that one dreams of seeing, or go through the entire collection and therefore the history of, say, impressionist painting, and in so doing locate the evolution of that art movement and the repository of human thought it represents.

One can also cross cultures and time. Look first at Cyladic art and then at African art and see surprising resemblances to that art in the clarity of representation that appears again and again in the self-conscious simplicity of modern art created by artists who might have been influenced by such originary forms of art making.

In this way the museum functions as a text that can be read—forward to back, back to front, or in excerpts. Focused as such, one becomes conscious of how information is organized. By noting what is present and what is absent, we think about the content of what the museum is communicating to us. What is the nature of our experience? What is the narrative the museum is relating? How does the experience change for viewers depending on their educational background, class, and race?

As I think about such questions, I note the pedagogical nature of the wall texts, how they can facilitate understanding or overmediate and intrude upon the viewer's perceptions. Sometimes such narratives recognize the ability of viewers to come to their own conclusions about the work; at other times they seem heavy-handed, condescending, or patronizing to audiences. I ask myself, what assumptions about the audience's level of sophistication do they reflect?

The wall text is often intended to help viewers access the work by decoding any encoded messages that may be locked within a certain academic discourse of art making. And at its best, it offers great historical information. But those who structure the experience for others sometimes seem to forget that visual work is made to be read visually. Many artists communicate their intentions well, without the use of language, even to those ostensibly untrained "to read" the work. Others are not as generous or successful. The goal for those presenting the work might be to achieve a balance where the work is given enough room to breathe and to speak for itself, and also, when it does not speak clearly for itself, to provide just enough information to allow the viewer to learn something about the work but to still have a real visual experience.

Who Made the Objects? Who Owns the Museum?

Art museums exist to preserve, curate, comment upon, and create interest in the history of art. Their main function rests in the curatorial and archival exhibition of artwork, so they are in the constant process of acquiring new works of art to strengthen their collections. Museums can deaccession art with the approval of the board of trustees, and usually when they do they acquire new works as they try to improve their holdings. The Art Institute's greatness, for example, lies in its collections of European, American, and Asian paintings, sculpture, design, and decorative arts. There always are selections from the permanent collection on display as well as new temporary exhibitions. With its own exhibitions, the museum hopes to enrich international curatorial practice, attract the public to its doors, and thereby help to increase revenues.

Most museums charge entrance fees, although there are free days open to the public, and many receive city subsidies because, as in the Art Institute's case, they are often located on public land. But most museums are no longer financially viable. The curatorial departments of museums often run deficits and look to the restaurants, stores, special events, grant opportunities, and donors to defray the exorbitant costs of mounting exhibitions. Most museums' guidelines stipulate that under no circumstances can they deaccession art to pay operating costs. Museums can sell art only to buy more art.

As a result, museums are profoundly dependent on donations, endowments, and gifts of art from wealthy donors—including relying on this class of people to bequeath them their private collections. One benefit for such patrons is that sometimes they are immortalized when a wing or a section of the museum bears their name.

In Carol Duncan's book *Civilizing Rituals,* a definitive study of the origins of so-called "public museums," she writes about such complex relationships in her descriptions of the way in which wings were added to the Metropolitan Museum of Art and the memorializing rituals, as she calls them, that such additions represent.[5] But none of her descriptions and concerns for the privatized nature of such "public space" resonates as profoundly as her chronology of how the Mellon collection became the center of the National Gallery in Washington, which to this day is assumed by most to have been a government-instituted collection. Duncan writes:

Along with Andrew Carnegie, John D. Rockefeller, and J.P. Morgan, Andrew W. Mellon (1855–1937) was one of the handful of men who shaped the U.S. economy at the turn of the century.... Mellon started out hugely rich and became increasingly richer. By 1920 he controlled one of the nation's two or three biggest fortunes, which included enormous holdings in aluminum, oil, railroads, and coal.[6]

Mellon entered political life in 1921 and served as secretary of the treasury until the prosperity of the 1920s came crashing to a halt with the Depression of the 1930s. During his successful years, he began to amass a significant personal art collection "in the hope," as he reportedly said, of linking himself with "something eternal." In 1936, when he fell out of favor and was forced to leave public office, he wrote to Franklin Roosevelt and offered his paintings as a "nucleus of a national collection.... His offer included a building to house the collection and an endowment for its development."[7] Other offers of collections soon followed, and a neoclassical marble building, "both solemn and tomb-like,"[8] was built in Washington.

Such is a saga familiar to America and increasingly also to Europe and Asia: The rich business tycoon at some point becomes interested in building another kind of fortune—the fortune of art. Sometimes this association with art becomes a way of laundering a somewhat sullied reputation. Often such institutions serve a particular class of people and their interests, and although these institutions may present themselves as tributes to democracy and egalitarianism, in fact they have been, and continue to be, structured around the goals, desires, and aspirations of an exceedingly wealthy class of patrons. This dynamic greatly affects who has intellectual access to museums and who can influence museums' missions.

In *The Field of Cultural Production*, Bourdieu describes how public museums, which appear to be open to all, structurally exclude those who cannot bring adequate "cultural capital" to them. In the introduction, Randall Johnson writes:

> Bourdieu defines cultural capital as a form of knowledge, an internalized code or a cognitive acquisition which equips the social agent with empathy towards, appreciation for, or competence in deciphering cultural relations and cultural artifacts. He suggests that "a work of art has meaning and interest only for someone who possesses the cultural competence, that is, the code into which it is encoded."[9]

American museums' collections are dominated by an imported body of European art, which is unfamiliar to Americans who have not been educated in the history of such art. The numbers of such uninformed viewers are on the rise, as public school systems increasingly lack instruction in art and art history. For Europeans, such work is part of the national patrimony and is often known to many, so when they enter the museum they are culturally at home. Such knowledge in the United States has become associated with the taste and privilege of an affluent class with a particular background. Because of the large cultural mix that comprises U.S. society, some of those who have immigrated to the United States are quite familiar with other bodies of cultural knowledge, not always adequately represented in U.S. public museums. In America, since art history often means European art history and because a breadth of such knowledge is often only acquired by a few, it is not surprising, writes Randall Johnson, that "regular museum attendance increases with increasing levels of education, to the point where, although theoretically open to all, art museums become 'almost the exclusive domain of the cultivated classes.' They have all the outward appearances of legitimacy, since the only ones excluded are those who exclude themselves."[10] And Bourdieu writes, "Museums betray, in their smallest details of the morphology and organization, their true function, which is to strengthen the feeling of belonging in some and the feeling of exclusion in others."[11]

Which Class? Which Knowledge?

Let's add to this conversation about cultural capital, ease, and entitlement a query about the place of artists. When my friends and I first discovered those dark galleries at the Brooklyn Museum, we did not know anything about artists. If you had asked us who made the paintings and sculptures, we might have said God. The thought of all that productivity across multifarious cultures was incomprehensible. Extravagant objects from Africa and the excesses of European decorative arts were equally unknown to us. As is true of most people, we became familiar with the objects but had almost no idea about the process of their creation.

Of all groups associated with museums, it would seem that those who make the objects housed therein should be the most comfortable in such institutions and, if not comfortable, then the most inherently admired. But they are not. It would also seem that art schools, the place where artists are educated, would also have a very vital connection to museums. But this is not the case. And it would seem that both artists and art schools would have a great deal of cultural capital in relationship to museums, but they do not.

From the outside, it would appear that the relationship between a school and a museum would make perfect sense. But this type of connection has never been easily understood. For example, the School of the Art Institute of Chicago was founded in 1866 as the Chicago Academy of Design. It became the Chicago Academy of Fine Arts in 1879. At that time there was the desire to build a collection, and in 1882 this entity, which combined the already existing school with the museum, became known as the Art Institute of Chicago. Few recognize that the school came before the museum. The museum was founded to provide a research collection for the school and to house its objects. Of course, such a chronology makes sense: First there are artists, then there is art, and still later there is a need to protect and display the art that has been produced.

Institutions combining such schools with museums were nineteenth-century constructs long since abandoned. Those few entities like that in Chicago—the Corcoran College of Art and Design in Washington, D.C., and the Boston Museum School—originated at that time. No one has invented a new version of this for some time. The connection between a school and a museum, which represents the relationship between artists and the presentation of the objects they create, is a precarious one at best. In the written history of the School of the Art Institute up to 1981, it is clear that soon after the school and museum became one institution, the trustees of the Art Institute quickly lost interest in maintaining a school, which for many of them was far more complex and less compelling than the maintenance and presentation of the objects. The history of the School of the Art Institute is a testimony to its resilience—its ability to build a superb educational environment and maintain a great reputation in spite of a certain second-class status within this corporate structure, although by the 1990s the school's budget exceeded that of the museum's, and the school's reputation soared. Why does such a disconnect exist between the repositories of art—museums—and those who actually make the work that is then collected? The way in which art schools are misunderstood may have something to do with this enigma.

Within the elite world of historical museums, art schools have little cachet. In certain contexts, art schools are seen as trade schools. For example, the National Endowment for the Humanities grant office positions art schools in the same category as specialized engineering schools. Several prestigious art programs in major universities are located in the same division as nursing and education, in part because art training has traditionally been understood as a service profession. In universities, art makers are usually separated from the art historians, those studying exhibition and curatorial studies, as well as those receiving degrees in arts administration and cultural studies. Those who write and theorize about the making of art, as well as those who study how to position art in the world, often have little contact with living artists.

I have met faculty members at the University of Chicago who, although aware that the university has an art history department, do not know the university also has an art-*making* department. Art making, apart from being understood as a service, also has been considered a craft, so it is often not understood to be in the same league as other serious intellectual work. Craft making, after all, is something that can get you dirty—not unlike, in fact very much like, manual labor. In this vein, artists once belonged to guilds and were often apprenticed to learn the trade from experts, and in some parts of the world (I think of my recent visits to Cambodia or the European academy model) they still are.

Art schools are the sites of art production and ongoing discussions about contemporary art. Here ideas are passed from one generation to the next, while new ideas come into being through practice. Young artists learn how to cast bronze but also how to program high-end forms of digital animation. They study the history of art from the Greeks to the most recent choices for the Whitney Biennial. And they learn to read Aristotle but also, and increasingly, Bourdieu, Derrida, Žižek, Virilio, and Cixous.

Art school discourse around all forms of cultural production and their theoretical grounding is comparable to that of the best contemporary literature or philosophy departments. And young artists are increasingly presented with a deliberately diverse curriculum that includes African, Asian, and Latin American art, as well as African-American, Hispanic-American, and Asian-American modern and contemporary art. And they are also educated to think of themselves as citizens of a global world.

Each generation brings to this ever-evolving environment its own take on contemporary art making. Innovations in technology now are cutting across disciplines, so we might see new uses for old technologies as well as new technologies pushed and adapted to traditional ends.

Art schools are more like laboratories or factories, involved in both research and production, than universities. Although artists deal in high-end thinking, they also fabricate objects or are involved in public practice. In this sense they do get their hands dirty, in many ways, involved as they are in green roof development as well as community politics. And although historical knowledge is being passed on from one generation to the next, art schools are so filled with constant innovation that the word "creativity" is rarely spoken.

This type of environment directly affects scholarship as well. Intellectuals who teach in such colleges and university departments are often influenced by this emphasis on process and begin to think of their work in such ways. They also tend to become increasingly innovative in the ways they mix disciplines and combine forms. Outside the traditional structures of the "Academy," they are freer to look at their disciplines in the context of all others and to challenge not just the content of the knowledge base, but the way in which it is presented. In such environments one is encouraged to break with the limited ways in which knowledge has been communicated in the past.

In art schools a community of artists and intellectuals are living at the edge of their particular disciplines with those who identify, at least in part, with the avant-garde. One can often recognize art students from way down the block. Experimenting as they often do with their own personal visual environments—their bodies—the meaning of their blue hair, multiple piercings, and tattoos, which might appear intimidating from the outside, might only really be skin deep.

In art schools connected to museums, this type of subculture not only comes right up against the ruling class, but ironically is also dependent on that class for some of the resources necessary to sustain this cutting-edge environment. The rebelliousness of one world collides with the actual and desired economic power, aspirations, and conventionality of the other. And although the art school, like this moneyed class, looks to the past and tradition for inspiration, its main currency is its hip coolness, progressive ideas, and place in the contemporary art scene.

So herein lie the complexity and contradictions of this relationship and also the obvious and as yet unstated collision between artists and museums: The work collected by and housed in museums is made by artists, a fact that is rarely discussed in museum circles. In the entirely constructed, repository-like, curated environment of the museum, discussion about artists and the process of art making are absent. From a curatorial point of view, it is understandably much easier to deal with art objects than with the artists who made them, who feel strongly about how their work should be contextualized and how it should be installed. This can create a tension for those curators who have a conflicting understanding of the work or how it should be presented. Despite such complexity between artists and museums, artists want their objects to reside among the classical objects they love. As difficult a goal as it is, artists want their work exhibited in and purchased by museums—the relationship that best secures its preservation, affirms its value, and ensures the artist's place in the art history of the future.

More Cultural Capital

At the School of the Art Institute an interesting tension exists when graduate students in art history and graduate master of fine arts artists enroll in the same art history classes. The artists sometimes envy what the art historians bring to art—the ability to talk, write, and contextualize art from a historical perspective. But art historians can also be jealous of artists, of their confident ability to look at and understand the work of other artists, the choices they have made, and the processes and intentions that engaged them. Artists, educated to solve problems in the visual domain, can have what is called "an eye" that allows them to see what is worthy before it is acknowledged by traditional systems of curators and collectors. Artists have a sophistication of looking and seeing that has been internalized and that is basic to what Bourdieu thinks of as an "aesthetic disposition."[12] He talks about the "naivete of the artistic gaze," as potentially the "supreme form of sophistication."[13] They also feel they have the right to comment on and analyze the intention of other artists as if they were interpreting their own genealogical line. They feel they belong to the same clan.

Whereas art historians and culture critics like myself fit into the category of what Bourdieu might call "artistic mediators"[14]—those who can ascribe meaning and value to the work, contemporary artists share with artists from the past the ability to create "symbolic goods." Art historians and cultural critics can comment on the art that exists and add a dimension of understanding to the body of artistic practice, but they usually cannot produce more visual art. Art historians possess the key to the "code" within which the work is historically "encoded" because they have created that code, thus giving themselves a high degree of cultural capital, but they do not possess the ability to make artwork. "Makers" can therefore easily diminish the value of their skills. Artists, on the other hand, have "artistic competence," which, according to Bourdieu, is a "form of knowledge."[15] They are able to do what John Berger suggests runs contrary to the whole contemporary trend of the art world, and that is to "see works of art freed from all the mystique which is attached to objects ... to see them as testimony to the process of their own making ... to see them in terms of action instead of finished achievement."[16]

Given these aptitudes of artists, what *is* their place in the museum world? It is not to consult with or help run museums. When artists do serve on the boards of major museums they are usually there as token representatives or as donors. Museum boards are usually comprised of successful professionals or their spouses who have the financial resources and inherited wealth needed to support these institutions. In such a world, where artists have little power, ironically the objects created by artists do. The artwork can move fluidly from one institution or private collection to another, but artists cannot. If an artist's work is collected by a particular patron, the artist may be courted by those collectors and allowed into the inner circles of rich donors. But when it comes to determining the future direction of museums, artists' advice is not solicited.

In the world of art making, however, the makers themselves are the most esteemed. And within this group, artists who gain critical recognition for their labor are particularly admired. Yet the value artists ascribe to the product can be very different from the value the art world ascribes to it. There is a great tradition of the "artist's artist" or the "writer's writer," referring to those who may not achieve critical recognition in their lifetimes but whose work is admired by those inside the art world for its artistic excellence and integrity. Hence the stories, strangely comforting to all who make artwork, about artists and writers whose names are now well known but who at one time had great difficulty getting their work produced or noticed.

In the world of museums, truly risky work rarely is shown. When it is shown, there is often opposition from the public or from the institution's board. This is even true of contemporary museums. Work shown in such spaces usually has already received art world imprimatur. This often means that when work is new and truly exciting, it is excluded from the establishment until it goes through a process of validation. But by then its moment of contemporary relevance has usually passed.

In 2003 a storm swirled around the Museum of Contemporary Art in Chicago because of a piece in a show curated by Michael Rooks called "War (What Is It Good For?)."[17] The video installation in question was produced by a group of students at the School of the Art Institute whose collective was called AER, Artist Emergency Response. The group came together after September 11, 2001, a time when they felt it was impolitic to speak out against Israeli policy toward Palestinians without being labeled anti-Semitic. Ironically, these accusations were then leveled against AER, the museum, and the curator by members of the board and the public.

The piece that was in question was called a "video petition" and runs for eighty-nine minutes. There are many different voices represented in it from the United States and Canada, people of different ages, races, religions, and occupations responding. Many testifying say that they want peace in the Middle East and that Israel must cease its oppression of the Palestinians. The video petition shows each person speaking into the camera making a testimony. All agree about the nature of the situation in the Middle East but not about the solution or the way in which the situation needs to be articulated. Many who are speaking in the video are Jewish. Nonetheless, Jewish members of the board of the Museum of Contemporary Art called the piece anti-Semitic and threatened to withdraw financing for the museum.

An incident such as this helps to explain why curators often fear showing work about contemporary political or social issues within a museum context. Because the museum's exhibition of such work is often seen as a validation of the work's point of view, those who do not know art well—and even those who do—often ask for another piece to be shown with an equally strong point of view to "balance" the original work, as if art could or should create a point-counterpoint debate.

In another instance of strong political work, the brilliant drawings, animations, and operas of South African artist William Kentridge, along with the work of many other politically engaged artists, had a powerful place in the struggle to end apartheid. Within its context and time, the work was deeply subversive. It spoke to the monstrousness of the apartheid system and to the particular angst of being a white, Jewish, South African male artist struggling to effect dramatic social change. But Kentridge's work was only really accepted in U.S. art circles after the end of apartheid, when American curators were comfortable showing the work of a white South African artist. By the time the work was touring the United States on a grand scale, it had already been diluted by its American art world contextualization. It was still remarkable work, but it was no longer an integral part of a social movement.

As someone who tried to bring a show of South African art made by practitioners of diverse races to the United States several years before the end of apartheid, I know how difficult it was to gain the confidence that the work of Kentridge and other extraordinary white South African artists deserved its place in the U.S. contemporary art scene. It seemed that everyone had to wait for everyone else to say the work was significant, and this occurred only after the political situation was less highly charged and there was no longer a fear of showing white South African artists, even progressively politically motivated ones.

Museums are cautious. Even in my days of roaming the Brooklyn Museum, I was aware that what I was seeing was a refined world, purified, very different from that of my working-class home. There were certainly people with such "taste" in the Jewish neighborhoods of New York, but I did not know them. My mother had been educated only through the fifth grade, my father never finished high school, and their parents had not brought with them a cultivated love for art, design, literature, and music from Russia and Poland as some had. But I knew that this refinement did exist in other Jewish families of all classes and that it was to be found in places like the Brooklyn Museum. I have always wondered what children growing up in small-town America, without such rich cultural resources, did with their curiosity. But at that time I was yet to understand the degree to which the presentation of this knowledge by cultural institutions also affected how I perceived my own place of origin. Commenting on Bourdieu's work, Randall Johnson writes, "Cultural capital thus participates in the process of domination by legitimizing certain practices as 'naturally' superior to others and by making these practices seem superior even to those who do not participate—who are thus led through a negative process of inculcation to see their own practice as inferior and to exclude themselves from legitimate practices."[18]

It was in the space of the Brooklyn Museum and others like it that I became aware that as rich as my ethnic families were in folkloric traditions, they were not "educated" according to a certain standard. And I became obsessed with absorbing such an education wherever I could. Thanks to the nature of public institutions, I already had internalized my right to be in such space, but because this world seemed so much bigger than the one I inhabited, I wanted access to the breadth of what it had to offer. It is only now, after having received the education I so desperately sought, that I can return to where I grew up in amazement at how layered and complex my world actually was.

The Brooklyn Museum was an extension of the other sites surrounding it, all of which represented values I did not understand then, but I understand now, to be European—the Grand Army Plaza Library, the Botanical

Gardens, Prospect Park. All of these were nineteenth-century offerings—representing a way of life imported from Europe and Russia. These were part of how life in the city could be lived and why life in this city of New York could be so cosmopolitan.

Sadly, many of our European parents and grandparents never came to the museum. My parents, for example, did not feel at home there, and my grandparents spoke little English. Their lives—the lives of immigrant working people—were often not linked to such spaces. These institutions were outside their domain because of education, ethnicity, class, language, habit, or simply time constraints.

For me, however, the museum represented the entirety of "culture" condensed. I did not as yet understand that as amazing as the Brooklyn Museum was, it too suffered the hierarchies of class and did not have the cachet of the Metropolitan Museum of Art. As elegant as its locale seemed to us in the 1950s, it was still not Manhattan. And as extravagant as its collections were, they were only a glimmer of what the world of global art making and curating had to offer.

Ascribing Value

Whether people attend museums or not, they often admire museums' objects, if only from a distance. Because a high quantitative value is placed on many of these objects, visitors recognize the enormous wealth embodied in such collections. Chicagoans, for example, have great respect and reverence for the Art Institute, whether they go to see the collection or not. They do not necessarily understand how value has been ascribed to these objects, and they may feel that millions of dollars for a Van Gogh painting of irises is excessive; but such objects command respect because of their place in the art historical canon and their monetary value. But the process of making art and the lifestyles that accompany and nurture it have not accumulated such positive colloquial resonance. In fact, often they carry a negative connotation.

There is the myth of the bohemian lifestyle associated with art making, which accounts in part for the "allure" of innovation and risk that accompanies contemporary art. This allure, in turn, derives from a mythology about the avant-garde—a frisson, a thrill—that allows individuals as well as corporations once associated with such work, by proximity, also to be associated with risk and innovation, in the same way that those who collect old masters' paintings can be associated with beauty and luxury. Artists themselves often buy into these mythologies, although they know them to be myths and are aware that such romantic notions easily can be used against them.

But once art is collected by museums, it succeeds in leaping out of the world of bohemia and the space of the studio to become precious. Then its conservation and its place in the canon are secured. But how the ascription of value by a small set of curators, collectors, dealers, art historians, critics, and auction houses occurs to protect certain objects is a mysterious process. This internal art world alchemy is not understood or even trusted by most outside the art world and is even elusive to some on the inside. Many artists themselves do not understand how it occurs or why they are included or excluded from it. Nor do they fully grasp why at times they are courted by a certain class of affluent people and at other times ignored.

In the art-making process itself, there is a complex reverence for and ir-reverence for the past, tradition, and affluence. Artists often choose their vocation because of beloved objects they saw in books, churches, public spaces, and museums. During the art school education, students connected to a fabulous historical museum will have the experience of walking through that museum with a faculty member who loves certain objects and is able to communicate that love to his or her students. Students will see and study these objects in real time and space. And they will visit these objects again and again.

For artists, then, there is this inevitable bond with museum objects as pedagogical tools and sources of inspiration. It is here that the work of art-ists of the past has been preserved and contextualized. But at the same time artists often feel a type of resentment for museums, as reflected by their austerity, sterility, and formality, qualities so different from the messiness and experimentation of the school and the artist's studio. At the Art Institute of Chicago, for example, an artist must cut through a certain amount of red tape to receive permission to paint or copy an object. One cannot simply unfold a chair and begin to draw, as is possible in many European museums. Here such activity is not discouraged overtly, and yet it is seen as a possible threat to the objects. And these restrictions give the impression that the institution is afraid that the process—the center of the artist's occupation—could be brought into the museum and could disrupt its static, stable world. And when art students propose to stage performances among the objects, this too is resisted and requires a good deal of effort to actualize. There is the sense that this repository of art cannot tolerate the making of art inside it, at least not by young artists whose credentials have not as yet been established, and that the making and preservation are two distinct processes. Although the school and museum once did share a building that had classes above the galleries, this is now no longer even imaginable.

In one example of the art school–art museum disconnect, some years ago we had a student at the School of the Art Institute who, unbeknownst to us, was adding pieces to the Art Institute's collection. He made replicas of small, cycladic sculptures and installed them on pedestals in museum-like vitrines. These were very circumspect, and it took quite a while before they were discovered. He had also installed faux humidity-registering boxes like those you see on the floors of museums. They were perfect replicas of such devices but were hollow, without mechanisms inside.

When we at the school first heard about these additions, we laughed. This student had not only created objects that could pass for the real thing, but, while hurting no one and damaging nothing, he had subverted the collection. We realized that his actions threatened the legitimate control those responsible for the objects must maintain, and of course these types of actions are not permitted. But on its own terms it was a successful interaction.

Soon after this event, I was at a meeting in one of the school's high-rise buildings that faces the museum's sculpture garden. I received a phone call from the woman who was then deputy director of the museum, who asked me to go to the window and look down at the sculpture garden. I saw right away that various other sculptures had been added to the garden by students—neither fake Henry Moore pieces nor, unfortunately, works anywhere near their quality.

Such events occur from time to time at the Art Institute. And when they do, the reaction on the part of the school is usually amusement. For a student artist to curate himself or herself into the collection in this way—a performance of sorts—is humorous, outrageous, and clever. But the museum's administration won't be laughing. We understand their response and their need to control artists and their objects. Although the cycladic pieces did not aesthetically disrupt the environment, they did corrupt the purity of the collection. It is this strong need to control the artistic environment that artists cannot resist unsettling.

But there are disruptions to the collection that are caused by the viewers, too. The Art Institute has fabulous buddhas and bodhisattvas in its permanent collection. From time to time someone will bring a small offering and set it at the base of a mount or in the lap of a buddha. I know this also occurs even more frequently in the Boston Museum of Fine Arts in its Asian rooms. Flowers, for example, sometimes appear at the feet of some of their most prized sacred objects. But the museum is not a temple, at least not this sort of temple, and although these objects are sacred to many, they do not appear there in a sacred context. Nor is the museum able or willing to convey the spiritual power of these pieces. I often feel these buddhas and bodhisattvas, because unadorned, become sanitized and desacralized. Like magnificent animals used to community who become isolated in zoos, they appear to be very lonely.

The people who leave flowers in the laps of these buddhas feel an affinity with these statues. The artists who surreptitiously insert their work into the collection also feel a connection to the objects. In this way, artists and visitors act as interlopers. One friend of mine took his entitlement to these objects to great lengths.

When this friend, now retired from teaching, was an art student sixty years ago, he stole a small Albert Pinkham Ryder painting from the Brooklyn Museum. He admired the painting so much that he felt he "had to have it." In those days the museum security was so lax that he was able to take this small painting from the wall, put it under his coat, and walk out with it. Years later, he wanted to find a way to give the painting back to the museum. A third party arranged the transaction, and the museum, quite pleased to have the painting returned, asked no questions.

This collection of stories illustrates the complex ways artists and others think about museums and the ways they attempt to reanimate the objects, neutralized by the nature of collection and preservation. To their credit, from time to time museums allow—and even instigate—innovative rear-rangements of their collections, and, when they do, the hidden texts of museology are often revealed. For example, artists like Fred Wilson are occasionally asked to come into museums, historic societies, and ethnographic collections and recurate the collection or parts of it, to respond to social concerns, contemporary thinking on museums and issues concerning race, gender, class, and so forth. He and others have made their art practice a reanimation of such objects through recontextualization.

In another example, three faculty members of the School of the Art Institute—art historian Lisa Wainwright and artists Lisa Norton and Frances Whitehead—mounted an exhibition located in both the school and the museum of the Art Institute called "At Home in the Museum."[19] This exhibition focused on artists' reinterpretations of objects from the museum's collection of European and decorative arts. They invited four artists to participate. Each responded to an aspect of the collection, and his or her responses were interwoven into the fabric of the museum and the galleries of the school. Mark Dion, for example, created a "Field Guide to the Birds of the Department of European and Decorative Arts" and used photographic technology as a means of "hunting and gathering images to cite instances where nature had been appropriated" and replicated onto objects. He recontextualized these images of birds as ornithological studies.[20]

Barbara Bloom set out to "make visible that which is normally occluded in the museum galleries: the object's shadow, its hidden underside or back, its light reflecting power, or the missing and broken bits of a damaged body."[21] She actually set objects in vitrines in such a way so that you could see the insignias on the bottom of the porcelains, or set them up in such a way that we were able to see the actual shadows these pieces cast, unlike the museum where you cannot turn pieces upside down and where the shadows are eliminated.

Josiah McElheny duplicated the size, scale, and shape of several historical glass objects but then transformed their colors and design, making them

Juan Muñoz, 9/14/2002 to 1/5/2003. *Photograph by Robert Lifson. Reproduction, the Art Institute of Chicago.*

contemporary in feel and allowing these "fakes" to draw renewed attention to the originals.

Some years ago the Art Institute mounted a fabulous Juan Muñoz retrospective. Juan Muñoz, a Spanish artist who died suddenly several years ago at the age of forty-eight, made fascinating work in which strange creatures inhabit mythical landscapes and art spaces to gaze, gossip, and observe. This retrospective was unique in that it was installed by curator Neal Benezra in conjunction with Juan Muñoz's wife, Cristina Iglesias, also a well-known sculptor. Rather than being set off in self-contained exhibition rooms, the curators positioned many of Muñoz's sculptures to infiltrate the historical collection.

The effect was fantastic. Visitors simply came upon these pieces while roaming through the collection. The surprise was in the strange appropriateness of the location for these unexpected objects. As if in a fairy tale or children's story, when at night the inanimate became once again animated, these sculptures appeared simply to have gone for a walk. But in this case these ambulatory figures, huddled together whispering on the grand staircase, were even more mysterious, because although they stood upright and migrated into clusters, they actually had no feet. In this instance the museum allowed the work of a wonderful artist to take its rightful place within the collection, not simply as a stand-alone retrospective but as an exhibition that reanimated everything around it.

Juan Muñoz, 9/14/2002 to 1/5/2003. *Photograph by Robert Lifson. Reproduction, the Art Institute of Chicago.*

Taken by the Light: Fort Worth, Bilbao, Milwaukee— The Unlikely and Untimely Museums of the Future

In the past decade we have seen various new museums constructed around the world, each with the intention of updating or replacing existing structures, or creating an entity designed to draw large crowds to art with what Michael Auping, the chief curator at the Modern Art Museum in Fort Worth, refers to as "celebrity buildings."[22]

These museums attest to the fascination with contemporary art—the new cachet and ability to draw donors and crowds. But there is no doubt that in each of these instances the building itself, and not the art, is the main attraction, and the art objects are at the service of the building—the largest sculpture of all. This phenomenon marks a new stage in the evolution of contemporary museums, one that will be analyzed for some time.

It may be that these new dynamic spaces allow everyone an equal experience of contemporary art by transmitting the thrill of the innovative, the daring, the never-before-accomplished through the excitement of the building itself. There is definitely a new sense of purpose for this architecture. The buildings no longer only create reverence for the objects or a sense of solidity for the class interests they represent. Nor do they create the sense of the museum building as a somewhat intimidating structure, a paean to "good taste." Rather, they elicit reverence for themselves and the architects who have created them. And if the gamble of their investment pays off, such buildings can generate great revenues for their locations. These new structures are light, transparent, ephemeral in their effect, and, at their very best, attempt to melt away when it is time to let the art take center stage.

A museum like Frank Gehry's Guggenheim Bilbao, for example, was conceptualized to transform a depressed industrial city in Spain's Basque region into a new destination for global culture. This strategy to attract visitors to both the museum and the city also was true for the new Santiago Calatrava addition to the Milwaukee Art Museum. In another example, the new Tadao Ando building for the Modern Art Museum of Fort Worth has been touted as one of the most elegantly designed new constructions yet actualized. Here the curators sought to create an environment so spectacular, so exciting that not only would it draw thousands of visitors a day, as it has, but it would also be an ideal venue in which to see contemporary art. Michael Auping said, "If a celebrity building becomes a path to some greater appreciation of art—that's fine with me."[23] Like the Guggenheim Bilbao, such attention from the art world will help this city, which still refers to itself as "Cowtown," to reimagine itself as a cultural capital.

Some of the strongest critics of Gehry's building are artists who resent the degree to which the space overwhelms the art, or, rather, the way in which the space becomes the art, making the art objects almost inconsequential. Artists prefer a more neutral space—space designed to show off the art. At the opening, the only work that really held its own in this context was that made especially for it, like Jenny Holzer's site-specific kinetic sculptures scrolling the height of the space in several languages. Even the Richard Serra works looked too small. But Gehry's building also does not have the cold, static spaces that can intimidate viewers and in this way work against the art. In a certain sense, having the building as the attraction levels the playing field. Visitors needn't be art experts to be wowed and elevated by a fabulous building and to want to make a visit and inevitably also look at the art.

The nineteenth-century notion of the neoclassical building to house the European collection, and that collection, a reflection of the pillaging by colonial empires to acquire and possess financial and cultural wealth, is over. No one would dare originate such a museum now. All the rules have changed along with the new postcolonial geopolitical reality. The museums being constructed today often have a different intent and set of expectations for the viewer. These new museum spaces, unlike their predecessors, are intended to please, excite, and welcome, rather than be awe inspiring or instructional. One might say that, like art, they want to draw in and seduce their audiences. The Calatrava addition to the Milwaukee Art Museum is open to the public, not just as a museum but also as a café and bookstore. One need not even enter the exhibition spaces themselves to revel in the building.

The Future

The flashy new museum buildings change the museological terrain, but they cannot resolve the myriad complex issues museums face now and into the future. For example, as new art forms evolve, museums are having trouble showing work that does not fit into their traditional wall and floor spaces. At Documenta 11 in Kassel, Germany, in 2002, films and videos were shown within the regular gallery spaces. Bleacher-type seating was provided, and visitors could wander in and out at will. In the case of *Southwest Passage,* Ulrike Ottinger's amazing sixteen-hour film, it would have been difficult to watch it in its entirety under any circumstance. How can one show such work? Indeed, there were many complaints about the awkward seating provided. Yet the alternative, which would be to show the work in a theater with a screening schedule, also does not work. It isolates and separates film and video, the *lingua franca* of the twenty-first century, from other visual forms being presented. Such a separation seems terribly old-fashioned, as so much new visual work is multimedia, and the distinctions between art that operates in space and that which functions in time is increasingly blurred. The question of how to integrate the work effectively into a gallery context is widely discussed in the art world. Sound installations, for example, can easily monopolize a space. How should such works be presented and contained in these environments? And what about interactive media? The days of easier installations and silent static objects as the major curatorial challenge are long gone, while the notion of the quiet, still museum is constantly being challenged by artists' use of new technologies.

Another pressing challenge for museums is how to increase attendance. They are now constantly concerned with audience development, as they are in need of large audiences to help finance the increasingly prohibitive costs of special exhibitions. In this way, museums have reached out farther than ever before to their regular constituencies by attempting to appeal to families and singles. They have tried to "package" the museum in various ways, by, for example, encouraging visitors to attend specific shows or to see the permanent collection in new and different ways. And they have tried to create a buzz around even the most traditional exhibitions to lure in a general audience. Institutions that at one time could exempt themselves from aggressive marketing now have had to resort to it with a vengeance. They have no choice.

Museums also face increasing pressure from granting agencies to show work relevant to a broader constituency. To respond to this imperative, many museums have expanded the departments of museum education. In a smaller vein, curators also are under pressure to make artwork relevant to people's lives in more direct ways. At best this directive has resulted in more attempts to make the work accessible through various presentations and related events; at worst, tedious wall texts that overexplain the work and intervene in the process of the viewer's own discovery have emerged. This latter trend can have the adverse effect of turning off viewers who become aware, sometimes rather quickly, that their experience is being too heavily mediated.

In this difficult funding climate, art museums find themselves competing with other kinds of museums for the same visitors—with natural history museums, for example. When the Field Museum of Natural History in Chicago displayed Sue the dinosaur or presented fabulous exhibitions about the history and production of pearls and a similar show about chocolate, their family-focused promotions, not in conflict with their mission, were very well done. If you packaged art in similarly popular ways, inevitably it would cheapen the exhibition by communicating a false message that it does not demand a certain intellectual and historical rigor to understand the work. Yet institutions with very different missions are increasingly competing for the same audiences. This marketing conflict is also exacerbated by art museums' increasing reliance on corporate sponsors. As corporations try to use exhibitions to cleanse their images and get their name on every public billboard, it becomes harder and harder not to see big museum shows as Disney-fied versions of art encounters.

In reference to the aforementioned strategy to lure new visitors with exciting new architecture, we have to ask: Will viewers come back to Bilbao or Fort Worth after having seen the buildings once? Maybe museums positioned as global attractions will only sustain themselves in this way for a time. Will local audiences also be seduced to visit them over and over again? We already know that this has not happened in Bilbao, where local residents for the most part are uninterested in the museum and the work it shows, since it often has little to do with Basque culture. Will a moment come when all those who want to see Gehry's building will have done so? When that day arrives, will people still travel from all over to this rather remote city just to look at contemporary art?

In the end, the relevance of art to people's daily lives needs to be reaffirmed and reconceptualized if the function of museums to preserve and exhibit objects is to continue. Generations like mine that revered static objects presented in classical ways will not be with us forever. And as magical as the silence of museums can be, enticing the next generations of visitors and donors raised with very different sensibilities and desires in relationship to art will take considerable imagination.

We can only speculate how future audiences for art might be configured if, for example, children in the United States were given sufficient educational tools in the public school systems to enable them to approach artistic work with confidence. Until this educational goal is met, there will be an inevitable perpetuation of class intimidation that affects who will go to museums, feel at home in them, and find relevance in what they see there after they are on their own, and no longer summoned to them by their educational institutions.

Given all these challenges, including the ubiquity of technology and the precarious future art at times may seem to have in U.S. society, more creative young people now seek out art schools and art departments than ever before, more theorists want to understand practitioners, and more practitioners want to understand theory. And in spite of our recurring inability to conceptualize how to allow art to be as alive in its exhibition as it is during the process through which it is imagined, there are nonetheless more museums in existence, enjoying greater attendance, than ever before. Nonetheless, neither the traditional neutralization of work under the constraints of "taste" nor the desire to create spectacle that makes art more acceptable but threatens to dilute its power can ultimately secure an ongoing audience for art and museums. There needs to be a cultural investment in understanding how art emerges from and permeates people's daily lives in order to know what the future of museums *could* be.

Were museums able to reflect the dynamism of the creative process, for example, not only would they get closer to the source of creativity in artists and its embodiment in the art they make—its meaning and motivation—but they would also be able to show how creativity exists as a force surrounding all of us at all times, a force that artists, among others, have learned to access. Such understanding would help to explain the power artists have, which is neither the force of money, class, nor social influence—those aspects traditionally ascribed value in the museum world. Rather, they possess a facility for tapping into the essential creativity that motivates the evolution of human thought and action.

The excitement around this ephemeral process and its potential to imagine a different world could be unleashed in these new magnificent museums that are still searching for their true identities. Why create such exciting spaces and not have them sing a new song? Perhaps those who manage the museums of the future will want art making to come alive in their spaces. Perhaps they will want the experience to regain the enchantment that we felt as children in the Brooklyn Museum—a wonder so profound it continues to propel my intellectual and creative life. Perhaps they will encourage a healthy meeting of art historians, curators, educators, and artists to create seductive, contagious, risky, and appealing encounters for the imagination and the spirit, so that visitors once inside will no longer remain only in awe of the objects or the building, but will come to understand that the truly amazing aspect of it all is this process of invention itself, which they too can access, and without which neither art, the building, nor anything new can ever come into existence.

Notes

1. Theodor W. Adorno, *Prisms,* trans. Samuel and Shierry Weber (Cambridge, MA: MIT Press, 1983), 175.

2. Cited in ibid., 177.

3. *Webster's New Twentieth Century Dictionary of the English Language Unabridged,* 2nd Edition (New York: Publisher's Guild, 1967), 1535.

4. Marc Augé, *Non-Places: Introduction to an Anthropology of Supermodernity,* trans. John Howe (New York: Verso, 1995), 60.

5. Carol Duncan, *Civilizing Rituals: Inside Public Art Museums* (London: Routledge, 1995).

6. Ibid., 96.

7. Ibid., 97.

8. Ibid., 98.

9. Pierre Bourdieu, *The Field of Cultural Production* (New York: Columbia University Press, 1993), 7.

10. Ibid., 22.

11. Bourdieu, *The Field of Cultural Production,* 236.

12. Ibid., 23.

13. Ibid., 23.

14. Ibid., 11.

15. Ibid., 22.

16. John Berger, "The Historical Function of the Museum," in *Selected Essays,* ed. Geoff Dyer (New York: Pantheon, 2001), 94.

17. "War (What Is It Good For?)." Museum of Contemporary Art, Chicago, January 18–May 18, 2003.

18. Bourdieu, *The Field of Cultural Production,* 24.

19. "At Home in the Museum," curated by Lisa Norton, Lisa Wainwright, and Frances Whitehead at the School of the Art Institute of Chicago, Betty Rymer Gallery, May 15–June 24, 1998.

20. "At Home in the Museum," taken from the flyer about the show distributed at the Rymer Gallery, written by the curators, Lisa Norton, Lisa Wainwright, and Frances Whitehead, May 1998.

21. Ibid.

22. Stephen Kinzer, "Deep in the Heart of Modernity: Fort Worth Museum Frames Art in Wide Open Spaces," *New York Times,* January 29, 2003, Section E, 3.

23. Ibid.

3
Countervaillance
Educating Creative Practitioners

‑‑◇‑‑

What we call art is not only that which culminates in great works, but rather a space where society carries out its visual production.[1]

Sites of Learning

When people outside the art world visualize schools of art and design, they imagine students and faculty dressed in fashionable black, a factory-like production space reminiscent of an atelier, avant-garde art, and a hip glamour. Such images often accompany a type of magical thinking about how the transformation of young talented students into star professional artists and designers takes place. Rarely is the day-to-day work of educating the next generation of creative practitioners understood in its complexity and importance.

In these unique sites of learning, students come to master the visual through theory—the assimilation of art history and visual and critical studies—as well as through practice—the use of materials, technology, and technique. The approach to production learned early in these settings creates a way of seeing, working, and thinking that continues to influence artistic production long after the formal relationship with the educational institution has ended. In the West, these cultural environments have a long history of pedagogy that hearkens back to the early academies of Europe, where certain ways of working as well as implicit values were passed along. But today these environments are constantly evolving to keep pace with technology and the evolution of society in general. Their relationship to the commercial and not-for-profit worlds is also in flux. At the same time that they are influenced by ever-changing ideas about best practice and art and design theory, they also influence these worlds with the constant production of new ideas and methodologies.

Such institutions, with great aspirations for their talented students, appear caught in contradiction. They inevitably acknowledge and even encourage their students' involvement in the commercial worlds of displaying and selling art and design, but they also try to create a counter-environment that engages the creative process outside its suitability for a commercial market, at times encouraging students to work in conceptual or performative non–object-oriented ways for which there is usually little potential for market exchange. These sites of production operate with complex values—academic, even utopian in their belief in the power of art and design to transform the world—but inevitably linked to a marketplace that depends on young talent each year for its constant rejuvenation.

Understanding how such institutions work, what their values are, and how these values have evolved and affected larger conversations offers insight not only into the art world but into the dynamics of the public arena as well—where creative practitioners in democratic societies negotiate contemporary issues in multiple forms and locations.

Values and Attributes

What do the practitioners of art, design, and architecture, as well as art educators, art therapists, art and design historians, curators, and visual and critical studies scholars—those who comprise the faculty, students, and administrators of these environments—all have in common? I would suggest two things: (1) *visual sophistication,* a way of seeing that is very developed, and (2) a way of working that to others might not seem like work at all. Such practitioners live in the world of ideas and in the manifestation of these ideas into visual form.

One could argue that those engaged in advertising are also extremely savvy about the visual, using their skills to seduce potential consumers. But while practitioners of art and design also attempt to seduce viewers through visual forms, there is often, although not always, a difference in intention between these forms of production and delivery. Implicit and explicit in the education of artists and designers is an emphasis on using one's visual skills to further consciousness, to make oneself and one's audience more astute, and to help one's environment become more functional and inspiring. Of course many artists and designers do not function with these values in the foreground. But the educational process out of which they have emerged, if it was a true academic environment and not commercially focused, was probably founded on values more humane than simply wanting to lull people into spending more money, fixating on false needs, feeding destructive impulses, or developing an obliviousness to the social reality.

Those educating artists and designers, on the contrary, often hope to instill in their students a desire to create unique spaces within which the visual can help all of us recognize our deepest emotions, ask difficult questions, see reality stripped of illusion, and then gain the courage to confront this reality when necessary. Really good art and design should also allow us to understand that the imagination, when given space within which to expand, is able to experience its own nature as infinite. However the desire for material or financial success may ultimately thwart these lofty goals, these values make up the foundation upon which most schools of art, design, and architecture are built, and this is where the education of the practitioners of these disciplines often begins.

Play and Process

Fundamental to such creative environments is the belief in and commitment to *process*—how one gets from the beginning of an idea to its visual expression. Artists, designers, architects, and all who grapple with the development of ideas into form have a fundamental faith that if they give themselves over entirely to the process of creating, then an object, event, or environment will emerge.

How one creates and develops ideas is a very subtle, alchemical, impalpable endeavor and, like thinking itself, is a difficult one to describe. This solitary activity of allowing ideas to manifest as they choose needs to be nurtured and protected if one is to succeed in the arts. Almost nowhere else in the world of work is process, and the state of mind that enables it, so valued for itself—as a useful activity that needs no other justification. Creative people assume that, like the practices of meditation or thinking, the concentrated open-endedness of following the process of thought will lead to knowledge. For artists the process of thinking through the act of making is a form of reflection. And although process may at first seem like an inefficient, indulgent, or impractical methodology to foster, it is the only way to create the space-time module within which an unfettered imagination can experiment joyfully.

Play is inextricably linked to process, but for most adults it is perceived as abandonment of one's responsibilities, or at least a break from them. But for artists and designers, play is understood as serious work. Play is what the gods do. It is what mortals, at least grown mortals, are rarely allowed to engage in, and yet it is fundamental to creation. Play is the ability to abandon a sense of utility, to get lost in the present, to allow the imagination to roam freely and to be taken along its path without stopping to ask the importance, meaning, or usefulness of the journey.

In art making it can necessitate the willingness to break rules, trample conventions, and simply allow the whimsy of an idea to float because it seems exciting and brings pleasure. In nature, play can appear as excess and can manifest as extravagance or the unexpected. Why, for example, are there so many kinds of birds, so many colors, so much diversity? Biologists have speculated that one could understand this abundance of form as a type of play.

A sense of play governs artists' focus on process, but it also can animate the finished work. Works of art thrive when they communicate a sense of play, but it is not easy to play as a grown-up. Picasso understood this very well. People would often look at his drawings and comment, "Oh, my child could do that," to which the artist would respond, "Perhaps, but *you* cannot." Children give themselves over to their imaginations with abandon, but most adults have lost this ability, having become too self-conscious to be truly spontaneous. Artists and designers who capture the collective imagination for a time are often those who are most playful.

Part of the radicality of the design for Frank Gehry's Guggenheim Museum in Bilbao, Spain, is its use of materials. Titanium creates a luminous and unexpected surface for the structure that is particularly seductive because it sparkles and reflects. Such shininess, in the midst of the gray Basque city, makes the building feel playful.

The Guggenheim Bilbao. *Photograph by Manuel Blanco.*

The museum is breathtaking in its form and in its placement—at the end of a street of traditional buildings and on the water, which shimmers with intriguing images. It also is an excellent example of what is now possible as a result of computer design. When it was first built, it seemed as if it were the very first building of the twenty-first century precisely because it was so astoundingly irreverent of the expectations of its historical location, and yet it works. Good architecture should empower and enliven us to imagine the future and make our work and lives more pleasurable, functional, safe, and aesthetically engaging. It should encourage us to take risks, change the culture of existing taste, but also engage us in serious types of play. Most buildings do not do any of this, so when one does, it becomes a real attraction. Perhaps the inclusion of Jeff Koons's puppy at the museum's entrance should be read as a fundamental statement about the connection between this building and the notion of play. Why else have an enormous puppy made of geraniums standing guard at the front door?

In the mythology of art making, those outside the process often perpetuate a belief that artists *only* play, sensing the free-form nature of the creative process as quite a departure from most structured work. And artists themselves often feel conflicted and even guilty when they take pleasure in the freedom of what they do. But artists know that creative work of this kind is a serious endeavor and is often terrifying, as they face self-doubt and possible critical repudiation. Artists, like others whose work requires the risk of public humiliation, live in this anxiety much of the time.

When one is working with young artists and designers, part of the challenge is to help direct them through their own difficult moments in the creative process, when, for whatever reasons, they get stuck fixating on a sense of inadequacy. Their ability to navigate the turmoil and uncertainty of the creative psyche could be the most important skill they learn from their professors. These educators try to communicate that all creative people experience such moments, and that the ability to suspend judgment on oneself and one's work while following ideas as they evolve is the only way through these treacherous vortices. And even as teachers are reassuring their students, encouraging them to break through these internal resistances, they themselves often face similar fears of failure once alone in their studios. No one working creatively is exempt from such moments, but because they too are *in* the creative process, professional artists and designers often can help those just starting out.

Another way past creative fears and the barriers to creativity they present is artists' inherent passionate and fundamental need to keep working. For people in most societies the motivation to work is imposed from the outside through necessity and then through the demands of a job. These structures keep them locked into work, as conventions have determined. But artists most often generate their own jobs and projects, whether employed to do so or not, and therefore must be driven and propelled from the *inside*. Through the process of work, they are able to dissolve their own resistances.

Artists' inner motivation is something that an educational environment needs to help students learn to cultivate and negotiate, since it is essential for the successful production of work. Often such motivation is connected to obsession—the almost unnatural focus that keeps someone returning again and again to the same area of study, the same acts of engagement, until the energy for the project dissipates or transforms with the constant repetition and final completion of a body of work.

Faculty members at the School of the Art Institute of Chicago, where I was a professor and also dean for many years, often take groups of student artists, designers, architects, and writers on study trips abroad. When I first led such a trip to Southeast Asia, we visited Angkor Wat in Cambodia. This site comprises miles and miles of ancient buildings and temples whose facades have been carved over centuries with the stories of Buddhist classics, such as the *Ramayana* and the *Mahabharata*. Here a print-making student spent almost an entire week at one temple working on rubbings and drawings of a very small section of a corner of one wall's iconography. She had become obsessed and had narrowed the scope of the unmanageable scale of the compound into something she could effectively re-create in drawing.

In January 2006 on our "globalized city study trip" to Bangkok, Hanoi, and Luang Prabang, another student became intensely interested in the color of gold in Bangkok and in the sixty local Buddhist temples in Luang Prabang, Laos. He spent his entire time in Luang Prabang, the former spiritual capital, photographing gold ornamentation, gold leaf painting and adornment, and gold-sprayed stencils. For ten days he rose with the sun and the chanting of the monks and worked until the sun had set. Each student—artist, designer, art historian, visual and critical studies scholar, arts administrator, art educator, undergraduate and graduate student—had accumulated at least 1,000 images before we returned to the United States, and some had made video and sound recordings as well. Such are the passions of artists and designers: Once something grabs them, it doesn't let them go.

A high level of concentration and unrelenting obsession with detail, while trusting intuition and giving oneself over to the process of making, are some of the qualities that young artists and designers need to learn to navigate. These are also positive attributes that they can offer the world. By contrast, most of contemporary society tends to move too quickly, give up too easily, become distracted, desperately seek the new, and tread either too harshly or too lightly on the old to really *see* the obvious and the extraordinary in the ordinary and to locate themselves and their activities in the everyday present. The qualities creative people demonstrate may *seem* impractical in their nonutilitarian excess, but they are the most practical and potentially liberating of all if one is to achieve a creative life, accomplish meaningful

Relief detail from Angkor Wat. *Photograph by Carol Becker.*

work, and help to encourage the evolution of a sane society—which can only come into being if it is imagined. Jean-Paul Sartre wrote, "He who begins with facts will never arrive at essences."[2] Perhaps we can say that those who pursue a subject with passion, with the heart as well as the mind, and with the spirit of play always intact will more likely come to grasp it at its core than those who rely on information, quantification, or objectification. To transform society, one has to throw oneself into the experience of it in all its dimensionality. Otherwise its complexity will remain elusive.

Schools of art and design not only work to create environments that allow for and encourage such focused effort, but they also try to teach students how to create such environments for themselves once they leave, to set up their own studios and disciplined work schedules. Instructors, for example, rather than overemphasizing tangible *results*, the actual *thing created*, focus students' attention on the mode of experimentation, the conditions within which one is able to work—the questions asked, the methodologies employed, the state of mind achieved. This type of thought is often activated through critiques of student work that are intended to help move the work and the artist forward. Such environments also encourage a definition of success that signifies an effective manifestation of ideas into exciting forms—a definition not based on fashion or marketability but on whether the piece "works" in terms of its own integrity and the artist's or designer's intent.

In the larger society, value is generally not ascribed to one's progress on a creative path, the courage demonstrated on the journey, the level of knowledge gained along the way, or the innovations expressed. Rather, value is primarily attributed to the outcome, the product, about which the world asks questions such as: Is it useful? What is its monetary value? Who will respond to it? It is therefore often difficult to explain to those outside creative circles how something that has not as yet accrued value in the global economy, and that may never receive a notable reception (i.e., has not yet been deemed "use-full") could ever be understood as "success-full." It is also not easy to explain how embracing failure is actually *essential* to all unique achievements and should not be feared any more than the accidental or the unexpected, all of which might turn everything around and open up possibilities not recognized or understood at the outset of the project.

Students often come to schools of art and design having previously been in situations where they were deemed the most talented artist. At art school they find themselves surrounded by others whom they quickly recognize are at least as gifted. This situation can create anxiety. Some young artists and designers respond by trying to impress their peers by sticking to the type of work that previously brought them success. But in the art school environment, the pedagogical approach is to encourage the opposite: Unlearn all that came before. Start now. And don't be afraid to fail.

Communities of artists, designers, thinkers, and educators understand the value of trial and error, the need to fail, and that what at first appears to be an inconsequential element, an addendum of thought, might prove to be the most important discovery of the entire endeavor. In short, they recognize the value of a playful, boundaryless, free-form process. A designed object using robotics or electronics might not have achieved the imagined purpose, but it could take its inventor much closer to understanding how such technologies might be reemployed. Or the technique embodied in a "use-less" sculpture may prove to be a practical design component for a future commercial application. High-tech types originally conceived the World Wide Web as a communication tool to enable them to be in touch with one another. Initially no one imagined the extent of its potential. A painting that does not "work" visually, as artists say, could still be the most successful manifestation of an idea the artist has accomplished to date. Learning to make it "work" is part of the creative process and is a large element of what needs to be learned before an artist or designer can become a mature practitioner.

The U.S. market economy prides itself on risk and innovation, so one cannot say it is risk-averse, but it is *failure*-averse. In the United States we tend to admire and romanticize the spirit of adventure only when it leads to measurable success. But those breaking ground in any field of human endeavor know that without recognition and acceptance of the value of failure, there can really be no true risk taking, and without risk taking, there can be no innovation. In addition, one cannot live honestly as a human being and as a citizen of society, open and with a courageous heart and mind, if one is not able to admit when one has failed, either when it has led to greater knowledge or when it has caused pain.

At a societal level, the fear of failure is apparent in the United States. One need only look at the history of the U.S. response to Vietnam and the "American War"—as the Vietnamese call it—as an example. The United States clearly lost that war. But this fact is never spoken in mainstream U.S. media. It is as if the admission of loss might create a stigma from which the country could never recover, or the collective ego would simply crumble under the weight of this historical truth. The result of this failure of recognition is that the society has repeated its mistakes. For example, it has now become very difficult to speak the truth about why the United States began the war in Iraq. After the deaths of thousands of U.S. soldiers and hundreds of thousands of civilians, the collective ego cannot accept the idea that all these people might have died in vain in a war whose origins were based on deception and manipulation. And as long as the truth is not spoken, the reality is still not confronted. The societal consciousness cannot truly feel the magnitude of what has occurred or move on to the next level of understanding.

Accepting failure at a personal or societal level allows us to create different situations out of which we might better actualize our intent. These understandings emerge through process—through the space allowed for transformation and evolution, for the experimentation and criticality that, while leading us to admit failure, might just take us where we want to go.

Temporalities: Part I

Those who live in the world of art and design recognize that the most interesting ideas and work of a particular time often are not recognized as such in its time by laypeople and even by the art world itself. This is an important point for young artists to understand. They need to learn to trust their own abilities to evaluate the quality of their work and that of others in spite of the public's reception of the work. People educated to look differently, with great discernment, may *see* value where those with a less cultivated visual sense cannot. Over time, a larger group also may come to recognize the merit of something as the general level of society's visual sophistication increases and the ideas behind the work, at one time considered "radical" or even simply "bad," become safely absorbed into the collective consciousness. We have witnessed this phenomenon repeatedly throughout the history of art, design, and the making of culture.

When studying art history, it is surprising to learn that impressionism, the most mainstream, uplifting, sensual genre of painting, now broadly coopted by advertising, was once considered so scandalous that pregnant women were advised not to look at these paintings lest they cause them to abort. Even Van Gogh, whose magnificent paintings are now reproduced all over the world, sold only one while he was alive and that was titled *Red Vineyard at Arles,* and we know that he died penniless and forlorn. To recount this story is not to romanticize the inevitability of the artist as poor and starving in body and spirit, but rather to emphasize that in the case of Van Gogh the problem was never that the work was not interesting enough, but rather that the work was perhaps *too* interesting when it was made to be recognized as such.

In another example, Louis Kahn, one of the great architects of the twentieth century, died in debt and alone in Grand Central Station in New York, yet people now understand what an excellent designer he was and they travel from all over the world to see the Salk Institute in La Jolla, California, or the Kimball Art Museum in Fort Worth, Texas—buildings now deemed by many as perfect in both site and form.

It would benefit artists and designers to take the time to reflect on the meaning of these stories in relationship to individual lives and to their own practice. These true stories tell us repeatedly that success, as it has been defined in the art and design worlds for at least the past two centuries, isn't always the true measure of what is actually well done and important in the development of ideas. Rather, it is often an indication of what people are able to accept and understand at the time. Work that has been substantially ahead of its time or ahead of the context within which it was presented—years, even decades later—may eventually be recognized for its innovation and even regarded as a "classic." Originality and brilliance are historical and contextual constructs. The market value of artwork, translated for the artist as fame and riches, is often only attributed over time, long after the life of their creators has ended.

Some works initially fail only because they are not positioned within a receptive context or for the right audience, or because they are presented at an inauspicious moment. *Waiting for Godot* was a flop when it opened for its first American production in Coconut Grove, Miami, in January 1956. Starring Bert Lahr, who played the Cowardly Lion in the *Wizard of Oz,* the play was mistakenly billed as a raucous comedy, which set up a false expectation with a mainstream audience. The Miami production closed quickly. Produced four months later for a more sophisticated New York audience, who had already heard about the play's triumph in Europe, it was a tremendous success. When performance theorist Herbert Blau, then teaching in San Quentin prison, staged the play there in 1957, it was so well received that it helped spawn the first Prison Drama Society. And, in 2007, contemporary artist Paul Chan, in collaboration with Creative Time and the Classical Theater of Harlem, restaged *Waiting for Godot* in New Orleans in various outside locations in the Lower Ninth Ward and in Gentilly, recontextualizing the play in relationship to the desperation people have felt since the aftermath of Hurricane Katrina. Thousands of people came to witness the performances.

Artists and those who curate them often have their hand on the pulse of the collective psyche. In recognizing changes occurring in society before others do, they have to maintain the confidence to trust their instincts and not bow to what is currently considered acceptable. In a now famous incident, Marcia Tucker, founder of the New Museum, who died in 2006, curated a show of Richard Tuttle's work for the Whitney Museum in 1976 when she was employed as its curator of painting and sculpture. The show's reception was very negative. Most critics were simply unable to see the value of this quiet small-scale work, perhaps because it was shown on the heels of abstract expressionism, with its grandiosity of scale and aspiration. Tucker was asked to leave the Whitney, and the next day went on to found the New Museum. Tuttle is now considered a major figure in contemporary art. And the New Museum, securing its place for the future, has finally opened its own architecturally exciting new home in lower Manhattan.

Those who produce new works and those who choose to show them must be simultaneously very permeable—available, accessible to that which might pass through them—and tough enough to withstand the rejection expressed in word, deed, and limited compensation that might be short term or might last a lifetime. They need to cultivate a true independence of mind so they can weather the opinions of others who may have a less sophisticated or less daring sensibility.

Some of those who have gained great prominence for breaking ground in their fields may resist the innovations of others out of fear, jealousy, or insecurity and surprisingly stay wedded to the status quo. All of these situations, and the underlying tests of judgment and values they embody, need to be communicated to the next generation of creative practitioners so that they understand fully that the reception for their innovations, if negative, should not be devastating to them. Since these judgments will be dependent on the historical and sociological situation of the moment in which their work is being evaluated, they need to be able to distinguish this type of rejection from that which comes because the work is simply not complete or reconciled with itself. Nonetheless, it is both the new and the rethinking of the old that comprise the terrain they must explore, no matter the consequence.

Temporalities: Part II—Artists and Designers as Travelers

Artists have often lived cosmopolitan lives. Even without much money, they have found a way to travel, propelled by a longing to see the great works of multiple civilizations that they have read about in art history. Within the world of educating artists and designers, there has always been a great value placed on viewing significant works in situ. One cannot adequately imagine painting and sculpture, buildings, and monuments from reproductions, and contextualization is crucial to experiencing what Walter Benjamin has referred to as "aura."[3] Many artists and designers also have felt a kinship with other practitioners across cultures, finding in the work of other civilizations similar goals, methodologies, and often an even more innovative visual acuity. This has propelled them to spend time within other societies. But now the urgency to understand how art and artists, design and designers fit into multiple societies has become even more essential.

If young artists and designers are to be useful to this historical time, they need to understand their own society and its complexities, but they also need to comprehend a much broader, global concept of society, where they fit within it, what they might add to it, and then learn how they can move fluidly within multiple realities. Young practitioners need to be prepared for the contemporary world they are entering—a world moving so quickly where, at best, east and west, north, and south converge and merge, where cultures intersect and learn from one another and, at worst, where cultures collide, endangering the existence of all species and the well-being of the planet itself.

It is the complexity of cultural integrity, cultural hybridization, and cultural interaction that young artists and their professors must now consider. *Complexity* (densification) needs to be a core value embedded in the educational process. It is no longer enough to know one society; artists must understand multiple contexts. Most of us do not want the world to become flattened out or oversimplified, and there is a fear that globalization could come to mean homogenization. Many creative people find this idea terrifying and take inspiration from the places where the cultural terrain is thick and rich, which pulls them into societies other than their own. Young practitioners must embrace this complexity so that they are unafraid of the world's diversification and not immobilized by its social problems. While acknowledging the world's vastness, they still need to reproduce its specificities effectively.

I have always believed that the capacity to navigate this type of cultural layering, and not be daunted by it, is best achieved by travel. Young artists benefit from moving through different temporalities and forms of production. How else can any of us even imagine the concept of the global citizen and make it concrete if we don't attempt to experience the world's complexity directly? Writings about postcolonialism in Africa, Asia, and Latin America, while helping us all to understand the relationships of dominance and submission that were inherent in colonial structures and thought, have also made some creative practitioners too self-conscious to interact with these societies, as if exploitation must be an unavoidable outcome. Educators need to open students' hearts as well as their minds to ensure that they are not immobilized by theory. Essential as a starting point for understanding the historical dynamics of how colonialism and its aftermath have functioned, such theory, however, should not be intimidating or inhibiting. It should help to provide intellectual order to the oftentimes chaos of a worldly experience, but it should never take the place of that experience.

Artists and designers, many of whom are agile in their ability to admire and absorb complexity, visual and other, can become adept travelers and navigators of the "contact zone," the place where diverse cultures intersect, and are often able to transform what could be a barrier into a point of entry. "Contact zone" is a term introduced into linguistic theory by Mary Pratt to designate "social spaces where disparate cultures meet, clash and grapple with each other, often in highly asymmetrical relationships of domination and subordination like colonialism."[4] Where some may be resistant to Difference, or intimidated by the weight of history and its associated guilt and sense of responsibility, artists and designers as professional *producers* of visual material and also as *viewers*—the audience for the visual—are often inspired by cultural originality or specificity to make their own work. Whereas social scientists feel the need to re-present the entirety and complexity of societies, to acknowledge cultural relativism before they are able to evaluate and respond to different societies, artists and designers, having done their own type of research and interrogation, are often very focused and organized around their own interests and adept at trusting a personalized *experience* of place and then acting on it. Their enthusiasm for visual and performative traditions; their intuition about what might work as a creative response in a particular context; their ability, when captivated, to sit still, listen, assimilate, and transform can allow them to move within other social settings effectively.

Artists who have given these issues a great deal of thought and are willing to spend time within societies other than their own can create a free zone of hybridization, a place where multiple forms of cultural dispersion can coexist. They bring to these interactions either a consistency of media through which they have always worked—sculpture, photography, performance, film, painting—or a consistency of methodology, a way of working that is historically aligned to their past projects. Through this consistency of practice, they feel confident enough to take on the project and to locate themselves in its otherness. Finding something in the outside world that corresponds to a location in their interior world is no small matter. But it is remarkable that even young artists are able to do this, as I have experienced with students traveling in Southeast Asia and Africa.

For the past few years, I have been involved in a project called "The Quiet in the Land," which takes place in Luang Prabang, Laos, begun by curator France Morin. This project is Morin's third venture outside the traditional Western art world structures. In this instance, as in the others, she has immersed herself in the particular part of the world where the project would take place, preparing the terrain of Luang Prabang over several years for the project before introducing it to artists and before bringing a carefully selected group to Luang Prabang, a World Heritage Site and home to hundreds of Buddhist monks who come to study in this, one of the centers of Buddhism for Laos. As she had done in other situations—with the Shaker community in Maine and students and artists in Brazil—she brought artists into this complex community and facilitated their time in these locations so they were able to create work with and within these settings. For this project some very interesting and accomplished artists from various parts of the world spent months in Luang Prabang and during that time found personal ways of connecting with the place and its extended communities.

Photographer Allan Sekula, for example, researched his project by exploring the villages surrounding Luang Prabang. He broke his leg while moving between these villages when he tripped over hidden sections of barbed wire overgrown with plants. After this calamity, which involved being air evacuated to Bangkok for surgery to have his leg set, he completed his documentary, which begins in a blacksmithing village, Ban Had Hien, that still produces its own metal tools and utensils. The film focuses on the village but also on the devastating tonnage dropped on Laos by the United States onto the *Plane of Jars* and other sites during the "secret war"—the war on Laos. Sekula found a connection to the village through his own familial history—his grandfather had been a blacksmith—and through his own anti-war activism. And his film reconstructs a good deal about the effect of U.S. intervention in Southeast Asia in general and in Laos in particular.

Artist Janine Antoni sat in the Hmong craft market for weeks at a time attempting to learn the stitches the Hmong women use to make their unique embroidered designs on clothing, bedding, and objects. It was her way of connecting with these women and hence to the place. After establishing rapport, she collaborated with two Hmong women. She told them the story of the scars on her body, they told her their life histories, and thus a personal exchange was made. She traced the scars on her body and then reproduced the marks and the stitches on fabric that she asked her father, a former surgeon, to sew, as he had sewn her incision after operating on her many years before. For another piece, she traced her family's complex transmigrations through DNA analysis and represented this mapping pictorially using the medium of embroidery, a way of working that has great personal meaning for Antoni, since it is a form her grandmother in Trinidad had perfected. The Hmong women also embroidered elaborate depictions of their life stories—narratives of their upbringings, marriages, children, the war, and other tragedies. Their pieces and Antoni's were then exhibited together.

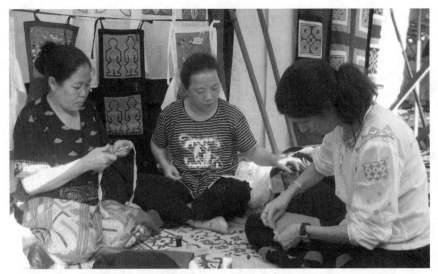

"To Ply 19." Artist Janine Antoni (right) working with Xia Xong and Moly at the Hmong Market. *Photograph by Paul Ramirez Jonas.*

Artist Nithakhong Somsanith, also a participant in "The Quiet in the Land" project, is a master of the gold thread embroidery technique that he learned from his aunts, who had created sacred stitched objects for the Lao royal family. After years of exile in Paris, he has now returned to Luang Prabang to work with "The Quiet in the Land" in collaboration with Vietnamese artist Dinh Q. Lê. Together they created culturally hybrid pieces. Somsanith used the same stitches he had learned as part of his royal upbringing and, with the conceptual assistance of artist Dinh Q. Lê, whose family came to the United States from Vietnam when he was ten years old, created contemporary images of Luang Prabang—beautifully embroidered houses on stilts with enormous satellite dishes on their roofs luxuriously represented in gold thread. Like Somsanith, Dinh Q. Lê has returned to his point of origin. He now lives in Ho Chi Minh City, where he works with contemporary artists, runs a gallery space, and continues to show his own work in Vietnam and in biennials and museums around the world.

Artist Ann Hamilton, whose hybrid practice uses landscape architecture, design, installation, and other methods while working closely with the Buddhist Sangha and with Lao architects, designed an elongated meditation boat for the monks to use as a place of retreat—an escape from the rapid encroachment of tourists into this small village centered around Buddhist rituals. The concept was based on the unique one-person walking meditation structures traditional to this Mekong region. Hamilton's boat was blessed by one of the most important monks, Phra

Acharn One Keo Sitthivong, and first launched in Luang Prabang during our group visit in October 2006 and again in 2007 for a second blessing in the presence of nine monks, nine novices, artists, and other supporters of the project. The boat was gifted to the Buddhist Sangha by "The Quiet in the Land" project, which has also raised funds to maintain it for some time.

As complex as the situation of entering societies not one's own may be, and as complex as the notion of cultural hybridization is, these artists' inspired creations and adaptations of traditional motifs function as transmitters of cultural integration. These hybrid projects can be "read" in Luang Prabang but also potentially in Rio de Janeiro, London, Johannesburg, Chicago, Montreal, and New York—all locations where hybridity is understood. The work can communicate in multiple settings because it makes the connection between disparate places and different times through artistic production while acknowledging and moving beyond pastiche, appropriation, the analytic, and the ironic.

Artists and designers are able to work successfully in places like Luang Prabang that are labor intensive in part because they so admire what local artisans, craftspeople, architects, and builders make. They are interested in forms of expression—where form follows function, and function follows form. And in most instances they are very respectful of the talent of the artists and artisans they encounter. In general, artists are not obsessed with the distinctions between art and popular culture, or with notions of high and low, art and design. Although critics employ categorizations such as these, those who create the work can appreciate the subtleties and solutions presented by many types of practice—objects and actions equally—unencumbered by a need to reify them into silos of definition.

In societies like Laos, where haptic production still exists, artists find inspiration from the respect accorded the handmade—objects for everyday use but also those intended for religious rituals. In Luang Prabang, where Buddhism plays such a prominent role, artists and designers can appreciate the abundance of iconography because they too live in a world of the metaphoric and the symbolic and are often intrigued by objects of religious significance, whether they themselves are observant or not. They understand that these objects have accrued psychic and iconic value and are often powerful as a result, and also because they have been fashioned by the best Lao artists. They also understand the hybrid nature of these objects, many of which have been influenced by multiple sources, including contemporary motifs and techniques from the West.

Because many contemporary artists still make things by hand, those living in societies that exist within exchange-based modes of production can appreciate the pieces fabricated by artists from cultures outside their own just because they also are handmade. Even if the images are Other to them, the art making is still usually rooted in one person's vision and is therefore intimate and does more than just reflect the anonymity of mass production accomplished for consumption. Rather, there is a recognizable and identifiable imaginative source for and meaning to the project with which they can identify.

And, perhaps most significantly, many Western and non-Western artists are comfortable living and working in the simultaneities of time, culture, and diversities of scale that one may find in such situations. As some artists have grasped, while traditional societies may be less technologically equipped to deal with twenty-first-century modes of production, they might be better prepared to understand its present complexities both spiritually and aesthetically since they are used to negotiating multiple cultures, languages, and religious influences. Luang Prabang is particularly interesting since it has experienced many forms of colonialism, including that of the French and the Americans, and has retained its Buddhist traditions in spite of its present communist regime.

Where might the respect for the handmade, the made, the personal, and the collective lead creative people? It would seem to direct them to a place where what many now regard as *retro* may point to the future—a way to proceed artistically outside the gigantic morass of the "market economy" to something more intimate and local but still global and significant, something of the self but also of the world, something applicable in both a society governed by advanced capitalism and one with an exchange-based economy.

There is an element of preservation in all these concerns, but preservation not just of the built environment but also of tradition. There is an underlying fear that not only will life on the planet change considerably if we do not become more vigilant about how we produce products and conserve our resources, but that the diversity of the world's cultures and the range of their unique production will become eclipsed, universalized, and homogenized if it is not treasured.

Sustainable/Unsustainable Practices

It makes sense that in the past decade the worlds of architecture, design, and art making have helped take the lead on what is now the very fashionable practice of sustainability. Although connected to the ecology movement of the 1960s and 1970s, this new iteration, which has taken form around issues of global warming and sustainable living and design, has become *the* movement of this next generation of creative practitioners. As a concept it also has thrived in the academy. This seemingly obvious and sensible idea is actually a very radical one. It goes straight to the contradictions at the heart of U.S. society and promises to have a profoundly positive effect on the future of civilization if we as humans can act on it soon enough to redeem, or at least to stop, the further destruction of the environment from human folly. It requires long-term thinking and planning, which in itself is quite unusual in many capitalist societies. It will only be achieved when people begin to think about these issues collectively.

When I was dean of faculty at the School of the Art Institute of Chicago, the school was closely involved with the city's project of sustainability. Chicago was one of the first to turn the roof of its city hall into a garden. Completed in 2001, it made a strong, public statement about the mayor's commitment to sustainable practices. Since that time, a number of roof gardens have been created, including Millennium Park. Probably the largest garden of its kind in the world, the park covers two enormous city parking facilities. At the School of the Art Institute we invented a curriculum called "The Green Zone," designed to capture the undergraduate imagination as it relates to these issues and to allow students to work on projects specific to the city—their immediate environment. As part of this curriculum, students, working with faculty, redesigned the signage for the Chicago River, offering a practical guide while presenting the river's history in a visually engaging form. They imagined new systems for recycling and created prototypes for green-roof buses, all in collaboration with city officials who were helping to determine which projects might be useful to the city, while critiquing their development along the way. These projects have enabled students to see the city as a location they can impact directly, thereby pushing the notion of sustainability from the abstract to the concrete. But the implications of sustainability can go even farther into the heart of a society like that of the United States than these project-oriented interventions.

If we take the concept of sustainability even deeper, we have to confront the most unsustainable practice in which humans engage—war. Measuring the impact of war based on the concept of sustainability makes logical sense since war is a strategy that destroys and wastes resources—human and other—in the name of speed and efficiency on an unimaginable scale that affects generations.

Architects, designers, and artists as a group generally oppose war and beg for other solutions to conflict. Creative practitioners recognize in a situation like the looted museums of Iraq the destruction of an important segment of art and architectural history. Once gone, these images of human conscious and unconscious aspirations can never be reclaimed. Like the human organism itself, which artists for centuries have represented in painting and in sculpture, the loss of even one person is the loss of a unique entity—an original construction that cannot be duplicated and as such is irreplaceable.

But when all else fails and pleas for peace are no longer heard, artists, designers, and architects traditionally have made serious work about what will be lost in war, what has been lost to war. Among the endless number of paintings about war and destruction, the most celebrated is Picasso's *Guernica*. Perhaps what is so significant about the effect of Picasso's image is that in the West, at least, it has come to stand for both the destruction of humanity by the irrationalities of war and the age-old longing for peace. Just a small fragment of this epic painting triggers a response, and one can see leaflets pasted on walls all over the world that use just a bit of this imagery to remind us of the horrors of war and ask us to stop its seeming inevitability. Lest we forget how powerful art can be, this image moved from being one young artist's response to the fascist decimation of the small Basque town of Guernica during the Spanish Civil War to become a representation for the universal catastrophe of war and its consequences, across civilizations, for decades.

During the Vietnam War, U.S. artists Leon Golub and Nancy Spero created canvases that became emblematic of the horror many artists felt in relationship to the irrationality of that conflict. They leapt into the catastrophe of that war—its ugliness and duplicity—and spent their lives focused on these and other difficult issues. Contemporary artists who see the unfortunate parallels between the Vietnam War and the war in Iraq are now restaging events of protest held during the 1960s as art pieces. We also see contemporary artists who have become obsessed with the imagery of this present-day conflict. Susanna Coffey, for example, has produced a body of work that I call the "War Paintings," imagery taken directly from journalistic photographs of the war. These paintings, like *Guernica,* over time could become iconic representations of both the nightmare of war and the desire for peace. They are haunting and apocalyptic, as if the world is being destroyed, and she—the artist; who continues to place herself in the center of the nightmare—is the only witness left to record the end of life as we have known it. Through her self-portraits amid the rubble, we are able to enter into, and perhaps take responsibility for, the nightmare. Surely we cannot walk away from, take our eyes off of, a situation as dire as this one for which there appears to be no escape. Or can we? These are dark, frightening paintings, unforgettable, reminiscent of Goya's Black Paintings.

One can easily see the art world turning its back on such work at a time when the *gravitas* embodied in much traditional oil painting is deemed unfashionable. But this response does not stop artists from working in this way, and it will not stop history from noting this work, when the smoke has literally settled and humans ask one another these questions: What was produced of consequence during that time? What significant body of work captures the devastation of those years? What were the acts of protest, acts of conscience? Where were the designers, artists, and thinkers? What were they saying about it while it was happening? Donald Sultan, maker of gorgeous singular images, often very decorative and derived from nature, has responded to the war with some magnificent and very dark images of displaced persons wandering along desert hillsides, blown-up trucks resting in rubble, beautifully executed and poignant responses to photo-journalistic images from Iraq.

When creative people recognize that these anti-war gestures cannot stop the destruction, some of them assume a different set of roles in society. They are often asked to help create the icons that allow society to grieve its own catastrophes. When we inevitably forget and do it all again, artists, designers, and architects build the monuments that commemorate the profundity of loss.

Maya Lin was a twenty-one-year-old architecture student at Yale when she sketched a design for a war memorial the likes of which had never been built before in the United States. Its nonrepresentational tribute to all who lost their lives has become the site of pilgrimage for the generations of Americans suffering the pain of the Vietnam War—those who went to war and those who grieve the loss of those who did not return. It may be the most successful war memorial in history. As a young designer Lin had the foresight to build something integral to the landscape and stripped of all heroic artifact, qualities that allowed people to see themselves reflected in the polished marble surface and to grieve unabashedly.

Another artist helping the collective to mourn is Ernesto Pujol, who began a series of "walks" in 2004, designed as sites of mourning and repair. They began as solo walks in cemeteries of fallen Civil War soldiers and are now epic productions using many student artists and others to participate in durational walks lasting as long as twelve hours. Performers are instructed

Ernesto Pujol (with Maria Gaspar), Memorial Gesture II, Chicago Cultural Center, October 9, 2007. *Photograph by Peter Coombs.*

in how to move as in walking meditation, and then to contemplate loss and mourning. At the Chicago Cultural Center in 2007, the performers grieved silently and publicly for the fallen soldiers and civilians in Iraq, while the audience did the same. These projects are of great interest to young artists because of Pujol's daring willingness to take on political issues in such a personal way within the public arena.

Fearlessness ›

The United States is in a desperate moment and thus, more than ever, in need of those who are fearless—not afraid to say what they see. "Preach the Truth to the face of Falsehood," wrote Herman Melville in the nineteenth century.[5] We might say it again at this moment, because we have heard too many lies. Deception will do to a nation what it often does to individuals—cause a deep corruption of the soul. Because artists and designers are unlikely to be given worldly power, in the United States at least, or to be tempted and therefore compromised by such possibilities, they often can live and work under the radar, as Guillermo Gómez-Peña says of the strategies of performance artists.[6] Because as radical and transformative as its work can be, only rarely does the society actually sense its true power; mostly it is hidden and ironically therefore free to say what needs to be said. In art at its freest we recognize its true potential—to show us how to love the things of this life, to abhor their destruction, to imagine what does not yet exist, and to refuse intimidation and the encroachment of personal liberties. These are the best values fostered in the education offered in schools and departments of art and design. These are the values many young artists and designers would do well to internalize and take with them into the world and from which they could define the purpose of their creative work and lives. If utopia itself is a site—albeit a non-place, not-place, an impossible place—then it is the site where such hopes originate and continue to live.

Most people, it has been said, live in the past, clinging to old ideas, to the familiar. Artists, architects, and designers, we are told, have the capacity to live in the future, dreaming it into being. But perhaps artists, designers, and architects actually live in the *present,* with their hyperawareness of what exists around them intact, always aware of the pain of the past but also able to *see* the opportunities, potentialities, and threats for and to the future. So perhaps they don't live in the future but rather in the *Now*—aware of the simultaneities of time and the relationship between cause and effect, seen in an instant and captured for eternity.

Can schools of art and design, with all their best intentions, channel this potentiality and make the prospect of social engagement exciting enough to compete with the versions of glamour and success presented by the art world apparatus to its constituencies? This is surely a worthy challenge.

If young artists and designers want to use their skills and talents to penetrate the joys and conflicts of society in whatever forms they choose, then the work of educators will be complete. They will have successfully ensured that the most creative people of the next generation will be on a path to what I consider success—the ability to live a creative life, making work in the most elegant, poetic, imaginative ways possible while participating in democracy as engaged and engaging citizens, committed to challenging its premises and advocating change, whenever and wherever possible.

Notes

1. Néstor García Canclini, *Hybrid Cultures: Strategies for Entering and Leaving Modernity,* trans. Christopher L. Chiappari and Silvia L. Lopez (Minneapolis: University of Minnesota Press, 1995), 176.

2. Cited in James Hillman, *A Terrible Love of War* (New York: Penguin, 2004), 16.

3. Walter Benjamin, "Art in the Age of Mechanical Reproduction," in *Illuminations,* trans. Harry Zohn (New York: Schocken, 1968), 217–51.

4. Mary Louise Pratt, *Ways of Reading,* 5th edition, ed. David Bartholomae and Anthony Petroksy (New York: Bedford/St. Martin's, 1999). Taken from an excerpt, www.nwe.ufl.edu.

5. Herman Melville, *Moby-Dick* (New York: Bobbs Merrill, 1964), 79.

6. Guillermo Gómez-Peña, *Performance Studies International,* "What Is Performance Studies? What Is an International?" Branislava Kuburovic, ed., *Performance Studies International* Web site: www.psi-web.org/texts. At this site there is an excerpt from a longer piece by Gómez-Peña in which he talks about being "an experimental cartographer," working in the spaces others choose not to work and doing so with tools others do not choose to use. He writes, "We theorize about art, politics, and culture, but our interdisciplinary methodologies are different from those of academic theorists. They have binoculars; we have radars."

4
Beyond Categorization
Art's Shifting Landscape

⤳

The Movement of Teutonic Plates

In *The Structure of Scientific Revolution*, Thomas Kuhn discusses the changes in perception that resulted from the paradigm shift instigated by Copernicus:

> Using traditional instruments, some as simple as a piece of thread, later sixteenth-century astronomers repeatedly discovered that comets wandered at will through the space previously reserved for the immutable planets and stars. The very ease and rapidity with which astronomers saw new things when looking at old objects with old instruments may make us wish to say that, after Copernicus, astronomers lived in a different world. In any case, their research responded as though that were the case.[1]

Looking at the same sky, with the same old instruments, scientists simply saw things differently. They observed phenomena they would have missed before their understanding of the relationship of the earth to the sun had been transformed.

It would appear that we are once again living in a moment of paradigm shifts regarding technology, including our perception of the acceleration of time, the eclipsing of space by time, and the transformation to a global society. We are so much in the middle of it that we can't yet imagine the discoveries still to be made or how they will ultimately transform our lives and how we think about them. Yet we do know that our universe has changed, even if we do not have the tools to measure exactly the extent of that change.

For example, it is not so much that certain processes are gone forever, but that the meaning of these processes has been altered—almost, it seems, overnight. The Gutenberg revolution suddenly made the mass production of books a possibility. Now, with desktop publishing, anyone can print a book. Even the nature of typeface has been transformed. Typed text from a typewriter now brings with it new meanings and nostalgic associations that would not have resonated as such even ten years ago. The look, the feel of it has shifted from ordinary to extraordinary, from the present to the distinctly past. Artists use the "look" of such typed text to a particular end when they want to conjure the past or the appearance of "low-tech." But before computers, typewriter type was the *only* look, the mechanized way we communicated with one another. At what moment did this change? At what moment did our methodology of working and communicating transform so that what was once so much the norm—the typed original manuscript, the long, typewritten letter—became archaic?

For many, the computer has transformed the art-making process as well. Not because everyone is generating images or text or both on the computer and thus making "computer-generated art," but because the computer has become an extension of the creative process for many artists working in all forms. New technologies, such as rapid prototyping—the ability to move right from an image on the screen to the product itself—allow artists, designers, and engineers to work in completely new ways. Also, these methodologies cross disciplines and bring artists closer to designers and engineers, and these groups in turn move closer to artists.

We can see how such technologies have already transformed the way artists work and think about their work. Some of the labor-intensive proce-dures, for example, that many sculptors utilized in the making of objects have already changed. The "handmade-ness" of objects has now become a vehicle for nostalgia. Even just knowing that there are such options has inevitably transformed how people think about making artwork. If they choose to create the work in the most laborious way, as many artists do, then that choice may become central to the concept and effect of the work. In another example, new technologies have transformed architectural rendering and building. Frank Gehry has said that his fabulous museum in Bilbao, Spain, could not have been built before the computer—he could never have rendered the architectural drawings for its construction before this tool became available to him.

It is fascinating to see the degree to which such technologies are being used by multiple kinds of producers. Students have become great writers of computer programs. A former student of the School of the Art Institute of Chicago, Paul Catanese, has written the definitive text on the computer program Director. Many young artists are self-defined "tech-heads" and are able to work at the highest levels with those programmers who are determining the future of virtual reality. The image of the artist, too, is changing. When before have artists played such a role in writing programs that are also used by chemists to do their work? Recent technologies have brought art, science, and applied art and science much closer together. Many artists, able to envision systems in space, have excelled in technology, pushing the already existing programs and equipment to perform higher and different forms of production.

Eduardo Kac is an artist who has received a great deal of attention for projects that push the limits of what artists can do with genetic engineering. In his most notorious piece he worked with French scientists to produce a genetically altered rabbit whose DNA was crossed with that of green fluorescent protein from a jellyfish. Alba, the resultant rabbit, glows green when put under blue light. This project was very controversial in France, and Kac has never been allowed to bring the rabbit to the United States, but this work marks just the beginning of the possibilities for artists in the field of genetic alteration—not only the manipulation of other species, but also of themselves. We have seen in the work of the artist Orlon an unexpected permutation of this, as she uses her own body as a site for performative surgical reconfiguration, striving for an aesthetically determined "ideal." However one feels about the complex ethical implications of such endeavors, their occurrence must be noted as remarkable. Their effects are still under serious scrutiny.[2]

Peter Gena, another member of the School of the Art Institute faculty, has worked with geneticists to transform DNA formulas from various diseases into musical compositions, giving sound to otherwise silent systems of organization and information.

There are numerous other projects bridging art and science, too many on which to elaborate here. But there are also collaborations among artists and environmentalists and city planners. In Ohio, artist Frances Whitehead and curator Mary Jane Jacobs have worked with a team to reclaim a site contaminated by acid mine drainage, transforming brown field land ruined by industry into a multiuse public park. Artist-originated projects have brought media skills to inner-city youth, like the initiatives of Street Level Youth Media, or billboard projects to stop gang violence originated by artist Iñigo Manglano-Ovalle. All of these use technology to some extent and create unexpected practices.

Documenta 11 took place in 2002 in Kassel, Germany, which hosts this international art exhibition every five years. It was filled with projects like that of the Atlas Group, a collaborative group that provides repositories for archival information and film within repressive societies of the Middle East. There is an artist collective that has been working to improve the water quality of the Mediterranean, while another artist group, called Multiplicity, has presented the information necessary to track the deaths of 283 undocumented workers who were attempting to flee their homes in Pakistan when they were lost at sea in a fatal boat accident.

Even as artists are painting with new gusto and hanging those paintings in museums, galleries, and exhibition sites around the world, others are moving further and further outside these traditional structures. There have always been artists whose work has extended beyond previously accepted categories. There are now artists who exist within the structure of their multiple identities as sculptors of public space, functioning as community organizers, instigators, interventionists, environmentalists, archivists, curators, and writers. Perhaps more than any notion of interdisciplinarity, there is an expanded notion of *art and artists* finally large enough to include everything that artists choose to address and all the ways in which their projects are actualized.

Orientation

The old does not work, neither does the new. Only a description of a transition.[3]

Perhaps it is true that we have moved beyond disciplines and interdisciplinarity, aided by revolutions in thinking and notions of practice and the ubiquity of technology. We are actually standing in a new place where we can see the extent to which ideas converge, reemerge, and take shape beyond categorizations, and even beyond the categorization of no categorization. It is not that form is an unnecessary consideration or that one can jump into complex projects without having developed a great deal of skill; it is, rather, a question of which skills artists now need and, perhaps most significantly, *why* they need them.

Art, like science, relies on research, experimentation, innovations in technology, and at times collaboration. But the difference is that art's object of study can be very subjective. It may be the world of dreams, the unconscious, social relations, or an imagined vision for the future. Art does not aspire to assert objective, verifiable, external truths, although, often and increasingly, work can be directly pedagogical and concerned with social reality.

But it is nonetheless true that even given all of this, there are certain paradigms, certain assumptions about what art will be, what it will do, and how it will evolve. When I say we are in the middle of a paradigm shift, I do so because the definition of art—the breadth of all those boundaries that once defined the practice—seems to be evolving in unpredictable ways. Even those categorizations that offer the greatest possibility for interpretation are changing, and we are not always aware of all the work that is out there redefining the limits and potentialities of an art-making process. Why is Eduardo Kac's green bunny an art project and not just a science project, since scientists have already made such psychedelic creatures in the past using fluorescence to track genetic combinations? Perhaps it can be identified as art because Alba's existence was conceptualized and initiated by an artist, and because her first public appearance was to have been part of an installation about domesticity located in a gallery setting in France. Her existence was not designed solely to further discussion within the field of genetics, but also to generate debate about genetic engineering outside that field. As such, her purpose has been thwarted, because she has not been displayed at all; the French government has forbidden her exhibition.

How do we characterize such work? As genetic art? As technologized art? As art at all? It really isn't clear. What we have is one artist's intention, while working in an unorthodox medium, to subvert through transgenic programming. From this we can categorize the work as another step in the process of art's evolution. In the study of biology, one observes how species evolve and cohabitate with those that have been in existence for some time to become part of an ever-evolving ecosystem. The future of art will be about a similar process of experimentation, germination, and evolution. Context and intention, more than disciplines, may now be the organizing principle within which to categorize art's multifarious processes.

Context

These phenomena are not happening in isolation. As some artists continue to focus on the specificity of space and locality, others define themselves within globalism—a world that has no borders. Indeed, the very notion of borders, like that of categories, has become the subject of discussion in many fields.

Certainly we live in a time of simultaneous information, and at any given moment we can be as upset about a terrorist attack in the Middle East as we can be about deaths resulting from an automobile accident on our own block. Most of us have learned to juggle these simultaneous realities and to move between them in our minds and actions, to live in a state of hybridity. In true postmodern fashion, many of us are no longer comfortable in any one identity but are accustomed with moving between multiple personas and identifying with various states of consciousness, as well as various ethnicities, organizations of thought, and physical geographies. Where we stand at any moment is a complex reality that theories of postmodernism have tried to articulate.

The world of art making has certainly become global. Documenta 11 was curated by Okwui Enwezor. A self-defined transnational, born in Nigeria but clearly a citizen of the world, Enwezor has lived and worked in London, South Africa, Chicago, New York, and San Francisco. He chose to showcase the work of hundreds of contemporary artists crossing multiple boundaries of presentation. Films were shown in gallery spaces usually relegated to painting and sculpture (art that occurs in space), as if film were just another form of gallery art. The exhibition was organized as if the gallery space were a theater operating not only in space but also in time.

The show made apparent the degree to which the art world has become global and how film has become the *lingua franca* of international art making. More successfully than any other medium, film shows the concerns of such artists on the "margins," many of whom are focused on issues of postcolonialism, borders, and migrations. Artists from these so-called peripheries, as well as those from the so-called centers, exhibited images from hundreds of points of departure. This variety of perspectives gave viewers the opportunity to immerse themselves in these locations and cultural differences, bringing them into multiple discourses, making them aware that their point of orientation is just that—*their* point of orientation—and as such it is only one among a million possible locations from which to depart. This type of exhibition reflects back to us the complexity of the art world and the complexity of this historical moment as we attempt to give it organization in our twenty-first-century consciousness.

The Complexity of the World: Space

Intimacy and distance create a privileged situation. Both are necessary.[4]

It is not just the complexity of the art world for which artists must prepare. It is the uncertainty of the evolution of art making and its place in the global order that must be constantly reevaluated. In this sense the *how* becomes much less central than the *what*. As the world, or at least an understanding of it, becomes increasingly complex, we must take responsibility for this understanding and our role in negotiating it.

The world in which we now stand requires us to be able to move both vertically and horizontally, in a way both deep and wide. We need to understand the dynamics of our immediate situation, the place we call home in the physical and intellectual senses. But we must also come to know the world we live in globally, the places that are Other, the *not* home. We need to be able to understand where we are in relationship to the totality, since our daily lives are so directly related to this totality—from the food we eat, the products we buy, the books we read, and the films we see, to the people down the block and to the wars being fought in our name. We no longer live in cultural isolation; all is interrelated. In this way we have become tourists, pilgrims, nomads, and travelers in our daily lives, even if we never leave home and simply—or not so simply—cohabit in urban life with people who have immigrated from various other nations. What is our cultural touchstone, or point of reference, if not this strange amalgam of familiar and foreign—the terrains we negotiate between?

We no longer have the option to remain isolated in any intellectual or practical way; everything has become hybrid, including us. We are impregnated with multiple cultures. Even if we only speak one language and exist in what we think of as a homogeneous reality, the complexity of the world seeps in, and as this breadth overwhelms and confuses us, it also enriches our existence.

What I describe is not unlike Polish theorist Zygmunt Bauman's depiction of exile. In *Liquid Modernity*, Bauman discusses certain writers who have lived productively between cultures—Beckett, Borges, Nabokov, Derrida, Goytisolo—and for whom the greatness of their work was very much dependent on making their homelessness a strength. "Rather than homelessness," he writes, "the trick is to be at home in many homes."[5]

For art making and for thinking in general, this would mean allowing oneself to be open to the influence of new ideas, methodologies, and practices, or to allow the existence of these new processes to influence one's thinking about the old and to incorporate the changes in perception that such innovation brings. This is what is meant by a paradigm shift. Unlike science, where a new understanding, once verified, must be accepted by all, shifts in the cultural landscape are more subtle, and contradictory belief systems may coexist. Nonetheless, there is a moment when most people come to share certain assumptions. For example, the understanding that the economic situation of the average citizen is affected by a global economy is now widely known. This took some time to sink in, but even in the United States, which is very isolationist, people generally recognize that our economy is dramatically, sometimes disastrously, interconnected with other countries' economies.

In other examples of art's changing influences, one does not need to incorporate the Internet directly into one's work to acknowledge that our methods and speed of communication have been transformed. And one does not need to invoke directly the look of computer-generated animation to know that it changes how hand-drawn animation *appears* or that *fake* hand-drawn is also a "look" one can achieve with the computer. One does not need to be directly influenced by performance art to imagine the act of writing as performative. These realizations have seeped into mainstream art world consciousness and have revitalized the creative process.

How one works and how one imagines one's work is dependent on one's own evolution and the shifts and changes in consciousness—local and global—that occur during one's productive lifetime. We see our own disciplines in relationship to other forms, and their qualities become more apparent, their reason for being *more* obvious, as we observe and revel in the multiplicity of choices that surround us.

Why does one choose to move among forms? At the moment we realize that to say what we need to say, to represent what we want to represent, we must cross between systems of thought and practice; interdisciplinarity has chosen us. It is not unlike why one moves between cultures and why those who do often produce such interesting work. Once one enters these hybrid terrains, prescribed set rules no longer exist. Although this can cause the anxiety of free-fall, we know that the most interesting thinkers have often been willing to experience this anxiety because they needed to say something that simply did not fit into anyone else's version of reality. This also has certainly often been true of scientists who need to break the rules, to burst out of traditional categorizations—with large and small gestures— to find vistas where they can *see* in new ways. This breakthrough process is both liberating and terrifying. It can bring with it rejection, humiliation, and isolation, because the collective consciousness often moves more slowly than individual consciousness. An individual can be way ahead of his or her time, and the world may not be ready for what he or she has to offer. We have seen this again and again in all fields of study. But exploring new creative territory can also bring great recognition.

The Complexity of the World: Time

Although it would appear that we all live within the simultaneity of time, our experience of time is often very different depending on what we do

Gerhard Richter, *Gegenberstellung*, 1988, oil on canvas, 112 cm x 102 cm. *Copyright Gerhard Richter.*

from day to day, our chronological age, and where we live. If we travel great distances and enter completely different cultures, a week can seem an eternity. If we stay home, the time, as we say, "flies" or flies away from us; we do not recognize its passing. Dislocation, putting ourselves in very different circumstances, can slow down our lives, or at least our perception of time.

When I was a child growing up in New York I would impatiently wait for summer to arrive, when all my cousins and I would visit our grandmother's farm in western Pennsylvania. We all loved the farm and couldn't wait to see one another again. If I knew we were leaving New York in a week, I would not sleep until we left. The week seemed to last an eternity. I became so obsessed that my parents didn't tell me when we were leaving until the night before, to spare me the anticipation. Now if I have a week to prepare for a trip of some duration, it is never *enough* time. I must anticipate not just all I am *going to*, but also all I am *leaving behind*. So the week goes by too fast.

Different art forms relate to time and demand our time very differently. If one goes to a museum to see a gigantic retrospective of paintings by Gerhard Richter, for example, then one knows that each painting will take a certain amount of time to absorb, and one slows down or speeds up depending on one's interest in each piece. It is up to us to determine how much time to spend.

If we see a four-hour film, like the Indian film *Lagaan* (2001), we are completely in the director's hands for the duration of the film. We have committed ourselves to observe the film, and the filmmaker has predetermined this work *in time*. His version of this story will take four hours, and so our participation will take four hours. A painter may imagine the amount of

Gerhard Richter, *Jugendbildnis,* 1988, oil on canvas, 67 cm x 92 cm. *Copyright Gerhard Richter.*

time a viewer *should* spend in front of each work, but he or she has no control over how long each viewer *will* spend. We are constantly moving between expectations in time as we observe art, each form demanding a different response in time, just as it does in space.

But the content of the work also evokes different times. It throws us back to modernism or launches us into post-postmodernism. We might even be presented with work, as I was recently in an art academy in Prague, that is the result of the most formal realist painting techniques, traditionally used for historical painting but now applied by students to contemporary issues. The effect is a jarring juxtaposition of style and content—a postmodern pastiche that creates a confusion of time.

The Richter show would probably include his paintings of the Baader-Meinhof anarchist group, whose members, it is believed, killed themselves while held in prison in the 1970s. The works are painted in gorgeous black and white, and the images were taken from news photos, television stills, and police files, to present a transposition from a familiar media format to the canvas. The result is a compelling, large-as-life retelling in oil of a sensationalist and very upsetting news story. The paintings move us back in time, making the past present, revisiting the historic event, reliving its pain. And the ephemerality of that reportage is transformed and transfixed through the permanence of oil.

Different disciplines exist in time and space in unique ways, and if one is trying to mix them, fuse them, creatively combine or reuse them, one must be aware of the complexity of their potential effect in relationship to time.

Simultaneities

We live in a social situation in which all these times and spaces exist simultaneously, and we exist in all of them through the ability of consciousness to move among various realities without physical encumbrance. When William Blake engraved images of Adam and Eve, Job, or other mythological figures flying through space, the figures did not have wings. In his mind they didn't need any. They were light as air, able to fly anywhere they chose because he was depicting their consciousness in motion, not their physical bodies. It was this lightness of being, not the gravity of material reality, that interested him. Yet the battle we are facing around ideas right now is full of gravity. That battle might well be understood as a conflict between the values of premodernism and postmodernism.

For some religious fundamentalists, the complexity of this world and its fluidity of multifarious conceptual choices presents religious conflicts, producing in them a desire to circumscribe and crush all such possibilities and to return all of us to a prescriptive, premodern simplicity that would be not only entirely regressive, but also intolerably repressive. The opposite of such repression of possibility is what Cornelius Castoriadis defines as democracy. He writes, "An autonomous society, a truly democratic society, is a society which questions everything that is pre-given and by the same token *liberates the creation of new meanings.* In such a society, all individuals are free to create for their lives the meanings they will (and can)."[6]

Here is a vision of democracy that is also a vision of art: Each individual creates, in whatever form or combination of forms he or she chooses, a meaning for the world. When all these meanings are combined, they become representations of the totality of the human experience at a specific time, and, hopefully, they also embody the moral and ethical goals of society. The multiplicity encouraged and embraced through art can reflect the best of what our human species—still in the process of evolving—might have to offer to itself and to all other sentient beings.

Such are the dreams of creative people. No matter what discipline or disciplines they practice, they cannot accept boundaries. But limitations to creativity most often are not embedded in the discipline or combination of disciplines within which we work, but rather in our imaginations and self-imposed restrictions. Yet, in spite of human ambivalence to our own potential freedom, intellectual borders are crossed and disciplines of study and practice merge and intertwine daily. Our job as cultural producers is to embrace these changes with the right mix of interrogation, rigor, and enthusiasm. At the same time, we must recognize that at the core of creativity is a blend of the new, the revised, the rethought, and the reimagined, all attempting to manifest the *what* through endless permutations of, and debates around, the *how.*

Notes

1. Thomas Kuhn, *The Structure of Scientific Revolution,* 2nd edition, enlarged (Chicago: University of Chicago Press, 1970), 117.

2. See my essay "GFP Bunny and the Plight of the Posthuman," in *Surpassing the Spectacle: Global Transformations and the Changing Politics of Art* (Lanham, MD: Rowman and Littlefield, 2002), 137–41.

3. Ulrike Ottinger (writer and director) from her 2002 film *Southeast Passage.*

4. Juan Goytisolo, quoted in Zygmunt Bauman, *Liquid Modernity* (Cambridge, U.K.: Polity Press, 2000), 205.

5. Bauman, *Liquid Modernity,* 206.

6. As quoted by Bauman in *Liquid Modernity,* 212. Bauman quotes from Castoriadis's *Le Délabrement de L'Occident.*

5
Where the Green Ants Dream
Aspects of Community in Six Parts

⬦

Prelude

The terrorist events of September 11, 2001, highlighted that differences in location, culture, and states of consciousness have made others "Other" to us and us to them. As we struggle to analyze the differences among humans—those within our self-defined communities and those outside, those who are sympathetic to a shared version of modernity and those who are not—we also need to attempt to remember the samenesses. Existing as it does in both all space and no space, our species's nature is utopian—of no place—yet omnipresent, an idea, a state of being so basic to our self-understanding that it is often ignored. Among the billions of categories of organisms that exist on this planet, from the cicadas in the garden to the cat sitting comfortably at my feet when I began working on this chapter, it is still with other humans that we share the greatest similarities.

Indeed, in addition to challenging our sense of difference, September 11 also changed the way we think about *community*. The word seemed to take on new and deeper associations, as New York City and the nation, miraculously, functioned as a community in the face of unimaginable catastrophe and loss. I try to remind myself often that my first and primary community, my first point of identification, is as a human being, and I agonize—*agonisesthai* (bring into contention)—our collective failure to acknowledge the most basic needs and sufferings of all humans. At the same time, I am always searching for signs of success—manifestations of compassion for our shared humanity beyond national and cultural boundaries, beyond locality, beyond an awareness of difference.

To approach the subject of community is to be thrust into complexity: the degree to which we are disconnected from so much of what defines individual societies—landscape, relations between men and women, indigenous cultures, language—and yet we are also irrevocably interconnected. Although we are unable to avoid the complexity of the world we have constructed, we are equally unable to avoid the complexity of ourselves—the mix of our contemporary desires with the longings that hearken back to other moments of societal development. When we speak about community, are we not really considering the following questions: What types of relationships with others in our species are we capable of sustaining? What do humans need? What is it that we want, and what keeps us from actualizing these ideals?

Traditional Communities: Dreaming the Past

While first conceptualizing this chapter I was living in Eressos, a small Greek village on the western coast of the island of Mytiline across from Turkey. It is also known as Lesbos. Entranced by village life and attempting to understand the meaning of my own atavistic desire to connect with the premodern, I have spent quite a bit of time in such remote, unlikely, but, nonetheless, often reassuring locations.

This village exists in two parts. One is the town of Eressos, a remote location made famous by the Greek poet Sappho, who lived here when in exile. The other is Skala Eressos, the beach town where natives and others go to swim. Some tourists come up from the beach to the *plateia* (central plaza) of Eressos for lunch or dinner—mostly lesbians from Germany, Italy, or Greece who are making pilgrimages to the site where Sappho once lived. The villagers don't seem to mind the presence of these women, who are often obviously in couples. Such otherness does not offend them. They are not it; it is not them; the differences remain intact but seem only to create respectful curiosity.

On a physical level, there is comfort in the size of Eressos, its placement on the top of a hill providing a vantage point for observation, the human scale of the buildings, the simplicity and uniformity of the structures—all white stucco or gray brick, modest trim in blue, green, red—an unselfconscious homogeneity of color and design positioned around a central plaza, or *plateia*, with four small *kafenions* (cafés) and *tavernas* (taverns). It is not simply the arrangement of buildings that is satisfying; it is the way of life such order reflects and facilitates: the bakery, the small fruit market, the grocery store all exist in proportion to serve the needs of the village community. This modest scale results in little waste. Each day only so much bread is baked, fish brought to sell, tomatoes or watermelons picked for consumption. When the shopkeepers run out of a product, it is over, finished, they say, until the next day. Only what is in season, only what can be carried from the fields, only what is desired is offered for sale. Everything is dependent on locality and physicality, ritual, and routine.

In the village, life is much as it always has been. The elderly are still integrated into daily life. They remain in their ancestral homes even during old age, with the entirety of village life surrounding them. There is public space where they can sit and talk—women outside their homes, men in the cafés. The villagers have the companionship of others from their generation and friends who bear witness to the trajectory of their lives. In many cases their children have left for the cities and return at intervals, for holidays, vacations, when their parents need more care. The villagers grow food in their gardens. Within this village population, among the constant inhabitants (not the tourist or weekenders from Athens who visit sporadically) no one has dramatically more material wealth than anyone else. If anyone did, he or she might choose to live elsewhere. The villagers share the name days of the saints and celebrate their namings together—Evangelia, Marina, Maria, all holy days. Even the village has a patron saint whose name day is celebrated with a festival, or *panagyri*. Here no one uses the word *community*. They don't need to. "Spoken of community (more exactly: a community speaking of itself) is a contradiction in terms," writes Zygmunt Bauman. "Organic communities just *are*."[1]

The village lives in a premodern condition, modernity and postmodernity move through it, but with one of the few Communist Party headquarters left in Greece, it is almost as it was fifty, or even one hundred, years ago. Only the hardware store has a computer to keep track of the movement of stock. What is comforting for the contemporary human organism in all of this? Probably the three things Bauman tells us humans have needed and continue to need from society: "certainty, security, and safety."[2] It is interesting to observe how these desires coexist in us, how the memory of such a life lives on in the individual and collective imaginations. The village represents a peasant life that many residents of major urban centers of the United States would find ultimately boring and isolating; yet most people would also respond to elements of its simplicity with a certain amount of relief. Many North Americans are descended from peasant stock. Although those who reach the middle class or above often try hard to dissociate themselves from these origins, there is nonetheless familiarity and comfort, for example, in not driving a car, hearing only the sounds of birds and goats, seeing a sky colonized by stars, swimming in clear water, and feeling safe to walk the labyrinthine streets any hour of the day or night.

As old men play backgammon and drink thick coffee—the latter a legacy of Turkish occupation—I listen to women speak of old age and their inability to walk as they once did, and I recognize yet again that the simplicity and difficulties of human day-to-day needs is here occurring simultaneously with the hectic pace of life in Tokyo, Bangkok, New York, and Paris, although the psychic space between these localities is immense. It is easy to romanticize the samenesses and the postmodern interventions that exist in all these spaces, but it is much harder to articulate the actual differences. So when intellectuals speak about the peripheries and the center, few imagine the distance that must be traveled between these spatial and nonspatial points of origin and destination. If one wants to theorize accurately about the totality of the contemporary experience, one needs to spend some time observing it, or it can be too easy to imagine that technological inventions like the Internet actually have transformed everyone's daily lives.

When we finally do bring our urban, modern, postmodern selves into direct connection with our own premodern desires for physical and psychic comfort, then we cannot fail to observe, as did Freud in *Civilization and Its Discontents,* that civilization, as it progresses and becomes increasingly complex, does not necessarily make us happier.[3] Since we have created this world in which most of us live in the West, why do we not make it more habitable, for everyone? Is it because we are caught by the contradiction of our bodies seeking safety in modest scale, silence, and simplicity, while our minds race uncontrollably toward the new, the complexity of culture, and constant diversion? Or is it that although our minds are comforted by such calmness, our bodies seek stimulation? Why, Frankfurt School critical theorists might ask, are we evolving a world that does not satisfy our most basic desires? Or are we just trying to leave the body—an unrepentant vestigial organ—and are stuck midstream, still daunted by its urgencies? Where is our basic species nature located? Can it be transformed? What will happen if and when we are able to supersede our own animality? What shape might our desires then take?

Artificial Intelligence: Dreaming the Future

It has become fashionable to theorize the "posthuman," but are we not in truth simultaneously fascinated with and also terrified by this notion? Who can objectively study the demise of our species, as we have known it, as we have lived it? The Spielberg-Kubrick film *A.I.* (2001) explored this concept in a surprisingly philosophical way, proving once again how film, literature, and art can articulate humans' deepest fears and desires, making them conscious and reintegrating them into our collective psyche.

Within the narrative, the corporeal yet ethereal creatures that evolve when humans have already become extinct, two million years after the beginning of the film (a time already in the future), emerge after the polar ice cap has melted and much of the world is underwater, including all of New York. This new hyperintelligent species has never known humans, so its members are very grateful when they retrieve a cyborg boy from the bottom of the sea where, miraculously, he has been preserved in a sunken car for centuries. Although he is not human himself, he *knew* humans and, most significantly, was created by them to simulate their image and desires. This new species, quite gentle and kind, is anxious for the cyborg child to tell them all he knows about human life. They recognize that even this child, although not of real flesh, still has residual desires programmed into him by his human creators. If they learn something about these desires, perhaps they will come closer to understanding the human species. With their extremely developed telepathic faculties, they can understand his needs by merely touching his head with one of their elongated, diaphanous fingers. Living as they do in the world of simultaneous time and space, they are able to offer him the actualization of unfulfilled dreams from the past. This cyborg child most desires his human mother, who has been dead for centuries. He is told that through their technology they can return her to him for a day. But they can conjure her only once. After that she will be gone forever. He accepts the terms, however brief, desperately hoping he will finally experience the joy of unconditional love, something he never knew while she was alive when she always favored her human son. He wants to be the truly beloved son, if only for a day, if only in a dream of the past returned.

Once the cyborg boy and his human mother are reunited, they have a perfectly intimate, almost Oedipal, day together, and she lavishes her affection on him and she does tell him how much she loves him. But when she goes to sleep that night she is lost forever and can never again be awakened. It is the most romantic version of human love—ephemeral, touched with the inevitability of loss. Merging two disparate genres—science fiction and fairy tale, one looking forward, the other back—the story is a fairy tale of the future, a projection of what might be imagined on the unfulfilled idealization of what never was. Here, in this Spielberg-optimistic and Kubrick-dark amalgam of a sci-fi film, even the cyborg body—it alone beyond death and destruction—is programmed with the strengths and weaknesses of human emotions and, as such, can neither be fulfilled nor ignored for very long.

Spielberg is hearkening back to the love of the organic when the human world he is projecting has long moved beyond it, or has used its ability to create cyborgs to establish new hierarchies—classes of beings divided between those of the flesh and those not of flesh. It is the organic that separates the classes in this future time when dominance, prejudice, and brutality still reign. But, ironically, it is the fabricated boy who survives and, more than all the humans in the film, is capable of deep love and affection. He has suffered the humiliations of human capriciousness and cruelty, but his programmed

91

desire for happiness through love, designed by humans in their projected, perfected image of themselves, has survived as an ideal for centuries.

What can we make of this allegory? Perhaps it is telling us that humans live at a crossroads, desiring the evolution of their own ability to transform the organic and rid themselves of the inadequacies of the body forever, while longing for an intimacy of experience still associated *with* the body and its vulnerability. When we imagine the evolution of the species, it is often expected that the inevitabilities of the flesh—its degeneration, decay, and ultimate death, its ability to torment us with pain and desire—will be transcended because humans, in the projected future, will be able to control whatever it will mean when we say *the body*. And we imagine that, freed from the biological body, we will also be free of the schisms caused by differences of race, class, ethnicity, and so we romanticize this technologically derived, seemingly liberated future. But Spielberg sees something else: What characterizes the species at all stages of its evolution is an inescapable longing for connection, intimacy, and community, all of which are often thwarted, while at the same time we are haunted by a profound insensitivity to the suffering of others who, whether human or cyborg, share the same desires and pains, whether they are organically or technologically programmed (as some type of "human") to feel them.

Spielberg is speculating on the future, and it is through a fiction about the future that we come to see the present—the degree to which we obstruct the possibility of community by replicating difference and maintaining the hierarchies of value that are used to justify brutality. As a filmmaker he is giving us a glimmer of how cyborgs might unbalance the social structures that exist. And in so doing he is warning us about how oblivious we are to the consequences of our inventions and what this obliviousness might mean for future societies.

Science fiction has always presented the future to talk about the present. And fairy tales have always looked to a mythical past to talk about how the unconscious clings to a lost world that tries to control the present one. What does it mean when such ideas are put into the public sphere—the place where individuals become citizens and as such ask difficult questions about society's direction? How do these ideas reflect the complex relationship of the individual to the society? And can we use public space (in this case created by a film) to help chart the evolution of the species and the progression of ideas about our own existence on this planet as they progress through art, popular culture, and other forms of social organization?

The Public Sphere: A Permeable Membrane

At this difficult moment in history, when the notion of space has taken on a new virtual dimension and time seems to have accelerated beyond what is healthy for the human organism, can we imagine a public sphere within which we in the United States could live and openly discuss the complex evolution of our species-life together? Could we construct a space in which individual desire could intersect with societal concerns and we could debate those issues around which there is disagreement? Complicating this imagining is that it is unclear what constitutes the public sphere in America or exactly where the line between the private and public domains is drawn. Bauman writes:

> It is no longer true that the "public" is set on colonizing the "private." The opposite is the case: it is the private that colonizes the public space, squeezing out and chasing away everything which cannot be fully, without residue, translated into the vocabulary of private interests and pursuits.... For the individual, the public space is not much more than a giant screen on which private worries are projected without, in the course of magnification, ceasing to be private: the public space is where public confession of private secrets and intimacies is made.[4]

If Bauman's thesis is correct, then democracy itself, which is dependent on the debate of public issues in the public sphere, is seriously challenged.

I'm not sure when I first noticed that the United States had become a society of confession, and that public space had been "colonized" with the "intimacies of private life,"[5] that politics was no longer about issues, that newspapers seemed filled with gossip posing as news, with celebrities appearing on the *Tonight Show* to tell the public why they were getting a divorce, and Bill Clinton, when still president, being asked on television what type of underwear he wore. At a certain point it seemed there was no longer a public sphere, just a private sphere relocated to the public arena. Maybe it started in 1984 when Gary Hart, then running in the presidential primary, confessed adultery, his wife at his side, on national television. At the time, many were shocked by what are now familiar, ritualized public acts of absolution. I thought, "To *whom* is he confessing? What community does he thinks cares?" If everything is now public, what *are* the truly private issues? And how does one understand the degree to which one's private problems are often rooted in social inadequacies whose solutions frequently rest in the public sphere? How does one make the link back from the personal to the societal? And if one does not, and if we do not, then what does the concept of society mean?

Most citizens are now compelled to seek "biographic solutions to systemic contradictions" and inevitably to "reduce the complexity of their predicament."[6] And such behavior can only support the delusions of a capitalist system that blames the individual for his or her lack of success and engenders citizens who do the same. Has the emphasis on the private collapsed the public, or has the death of the public—the residue of spectacle society—overemphasized the private and therefore overshadowed any sense of public? Whatever the origins of this situation, it certainly has successfully reinforced individualism at the expense of citizenship and destroyed the belief in, and facility and desire for, dreaming new organizations of society into existence.

The act of dreaming a future for society has slipped out of fashion. Postmodernism as a philosophical and theoretical movement in thought and art making liberated us from certain hierarchies of value that needed to be displaced, but it has also made the notion of imagining any type of cohesive future appear sentimental and nostalgic. To believe in hope, to want to conceptualize the public good, to value one's role as a citizen, and to believe in public discourse have all been labeled provincial or naive in this contemporary global debate. Yet without such imaginings, where are we—the human community—headed? We continue to want to talk about community within our new deterritorialized condition, and yet we know that the distinctions of inside and outside, private and public, so fundamental to our notion of community, are in flux. Bauman writes, "Once information could travel independently of its carriers, and with a speed far beyond the capacity of even the most advanced means of transportation (as in the kind of society we all nowadays inhabit), the boundary between 'inside' and 'outside' could no longer be drawn, let alone sustained."[7]

Eric Hobsbaum observed, "Never was the word 'community' used more indiscriminately and emptily than in the decades when communities in the sociological sense became hard to find in real life."[8] Or, as Jock Young writes, "Just as community collapses, identity is invented."[9] Bauman continues, "Identity owes the attention it attracts and the passions it begets to being a *surrogate of community*: of that allegedly 'natural home' which is no longer available in the rapidly privatized and individualized, fast globalizing world."[10] Surely it is this "natural" home that we all still seek, like the lonely cyborg child. Or perhaps it is a longing only those of us raised in modernism continue to experience, those who believe that there should be some place where we might transcend alienation and feel, if only for a time, safe and loved.

This new version of community that is called identity could be understood as that which emerges out of political conflict or repression. It could be understood as what comes after alienation when we separate from others of our species and make our difference our defining quality. Or it could be understood as what stands in the way of real political interaction or meaningful change in the social order. It could represent the privatization of the political and social realms, or it could be a transitional stage to reach the political in a new, fuller way, one in which all difference is included in the debate. Such disparate interpretations of identity are fought out among those who claim strong identities as a place of community, but the origins of these feelings, and what they tell us about the evolution of the nature of our understanding of community, often remain unarticulated in public space. It feels at times as if community as a concept has come to mean smaller and smaller units of distinguishing characteristics and histories, more exclusive than inclusive, and rarely moving the species out from these groupings to embrace a greater whole.

In truth most of us live simultaneously in multiple states of consciousness and identify with multiple communities. We are happy to acknowledge these complex identities and to find others whose identities also resist simplification. But in our need to cope with the ubiquitous nature of the global and our sense of impotence to affect it, many of us gravitate to more local, imaginable, and manageable communities. And so inevitably we land *some place* where we can negotiate inside and outside, private and public, self and other, individual and collective, a place where we can function as individuals working with other individuals to bring something larger than our circumscribed identities into existence. Having found our own point of location, we inevitably bring to it our expectations of what humans can accomplish together—and are usually alternately satisfied and frustrated by what we learn from the exercise.

Locating Locality

As the complexity of globalization, and one's opportunity for action within it, frustrate even the most sophisticated nomadic voyagers, finding a base that can serve as a platform for actualizing one's values becomes even more essential. It allows us to work for the present but also to dream for the future and perhaps to create an intentional community founded on certain agreed-upon principles. Of course, such self-conscious community building reflects the dynamics found in the larger society and therefore allows us to be more cognizant of what it takes to create coherent societies. Also, theorizing without a base can be dangerous. It makes us intolerant of all those who have constituencies to answer to and must, moment by moment, negotiate conflicting versions of reality. Praxis keeps us rooted—safe from hypothesizing in the ether.

The School of the Art Institute had been my location of practice for almost three decades. I did not set out to have the school be such a focus. Originally I came to teach literature and philosophy, but over time the combination of my own innate skills and the needs of the institution pulled me closer to its core. With others I entered into the project we call the School. During this period I had been able to observe daily what it means to negotiate a historically based community of creative people and to help dream them and it into the future.

In art schools, places where past and future interweave, idealism about the work that is being produced, the values embedded in it, as well as the way in which such institutions are governed are omnipresent. On one hand, such art-making environments are the repositories of tradition where skills and knowledge about art are passed from one generation to the next. On the other hand, they are places of great experimentation and innovation where leaps are made conceptually and practically, new forms developed, ideas generated, and cultural transformations absorbed—constantly. They are locations that help create the new but also are *unsettled* by it. They gain their identity in the local but are organically global—reflecting the international nature of the art world. And they create a community for many people whose unique skills are often undervalued by society at large.

Such institutions educate the next generation of artists and designers from places like Chicago and the rest of the world, and they also help educate those who will be the ongoing audience for art and design. Art schools also extend the notion of a creative community to those outside the institution who are interested in the artists, designers, and thinkers who are brought as visitors; the shows mounted in the galleries; the films and videos presented in the film centers; and the public intellectuals sought out for their ideas. Colleges and universities organically extend the radius of their own communities, creating larger units of those motivated by similar passions. In this sense, such environments reach out to many and serve their larger communities in ways often not acknowledged. What an advantage for a small U.S. town, or a large one for that matter, to have a major cultural or educational center as part of its core. How great are the advantages daily offered by these institutions to everyone who might want to make use of the provided opportunities?

But when there is controversy and work shown in art schools and arts institutions comes under attack, such institutions are thrust into another relationship with the public. Too often the response of the arts institution itself is to pull up the drawbridges and to polarize into the notion of "us" while the society outside becomes "them." The world is then divided between those who speak the language of art making and those who do not. The particularity of the artist's vision needs to be understood, but that conversation is often not possible once there is anger and certain groups feel offended. Yet the negotiations that then ensue are often not unlike those of citizens seeking equilibrium between themselves and the collective.

Such environments are fragile because they constantly try to create a certain set of conditions that will allow for the development of creative work, such as a certainty of physical and psychic space. In this the efforts of these communities mirror the stability that humans require from society in general. The academics and staff who govern and run the institution day to day must provide a place for the students and faculty that nurtures their creativity and allows for experimentation but also is capable of reining them in when they extend so far as to endanger themselves, those around them, or the institution itself.

Students are in school to develop their own creativity, but not in isolation. Their interrogations may begin with issues of form, content, or successful execution, but should extend to create a contextualization for the work that is inclusive of the history of art making, their immediate environment, as well as of the conditions of the world.

At the same time that faculty members are leading students through this process of self-reflexivity and helping them to develop a facility for making such evaluations, they are themselves also engaged in the same process—making work, evaluating it, contemplating difficult decisions, and putting ideas out into the public arena. They are also balancing the weight of the past with the discourse of the present and the risks necessary to influence the future. Art schools therefore resemble universities as well as factories, design offices, production houses, showrooms, laboratories, and galleries. Yet there is uniqueness in art school training marked by this emphasis on process and visibility of work at various stages of development.

It would seem that even the most creative people, able to envision myriad new forms and approaches to their own art making, should be able to create equally innovative, institutional structures to support their ongoing creative and pedagogical activities. But this is not always the case. Too often there is comfort in perpetuating traditionally perceived hierarchies between faculty and administration, as well as between faculty and staff. Unnecessary restrictions that attempt to privilege one form of art making over another, to restrict the movement of students within the curriculum, and to contain the physical environment in ways that are often counterproductive to students' creative growth also are often programmed into the structure of the institution. Such developments reflect a fear of the creative potential at the heart of the mission of these institutions. The contradictions of such unnecessary polarizations and categorizations often go unexamined, justified by a certain anxiety about the place of such institutions in the world, the place also of artists in the world.

And, unfortunately, perpetuated at times in art schools whose curricula are experimental is an infantilized sense of helplessness, a perceived inability to change structures to make them suit the constantly evolving potential of a creative community. Although intellectually supportive of the idea of removing boundaries, faculty members and arts administrators sometimes become frightened when the walls finally do come down. The anxiety often accompanying change and transformation exists in even the most creative people. In general, only a rare few are willing to leap into untested universes of production, and fewer still are willing to assume roles of leadership and then to understand such work as not only necessary, but also creative.

As a result, these institutions, which bring such play and innovation into the world through educating the next generation of artists, can miss the opportunities to bring the same energy to their own organizational structures which, if liberated from the weight of tradition, could add so much to the public discourse about leadership and pedagogy. From these environments, where governance, process, and creativity are central, we can learn just how difficult it is to build and sustain truly creative communities and to communicate their achievements to a larger society.

How can we develop creative leadership that encourages new concepts of community? What about those less tangible communities based on ideas and brought together outside institutions? Unrestrained by the specificity of place and tradition, what type of new terrain can they offer the imagination?

Ethical Communities

To the search for useful ways to talk about deterritorialized communities based on ideas, communities that take into account the contraries of the personal and the public, the local and the global, the human and the cyborg, the imaginary and the real, I add the notion of ethical communities. Such entities are brought into existence by people of shared values and are established around collective concerns such as the effects of globalization, world poverty, the living wage, racism, AIDS research and care for patients, restorative justice, global warming, freedom of expression, and the continued manifestation of the creative spirit through socially focused art and sustainable design production. Perhaps one is never so much at home as when in connection with others whose point of origin might be completely different from one's own, but whose deductions about the nature of society and its preferred values are at least very close to one's own. Such communities, founded around ethical evaluations of the necessary directions for society, might exist in what Buddhists call the "tenth world," the world of right now, the most present present, neither of the past nor the future, not bound by place, institution, or identity, and dreamed into existence to address immediate issues and committed to activism as a way of effectively mobilizing the world into action.

Together such groups could create visions of new futures—realistic utopias—able to incorporate the concept of the "human," which is being reconfigured daily, to move beyond those polarizing issues of identity that become new borders or roadblocks inhibiting the development of "species being." In this concept of species being Marx tried to encompass the full range of potential within which the species could best use its own capacities of reason and imagination. It is an important concept to bring back into discussion, because it allows us to imagine again the notion of the potentiality of the species to evolve. What are we capable of imagining and bringing into existence, not simply because we *can* but because we truly believe such innovations of thought will improve the lives of everyone? Peace movements, for example, have brought together widely dispersed groups of people who may not agree on much else but who share the goal of world peace. Environmental movements have done the same. And now, in spite of geographic distance, new types of unimagined communities have already been brought into existence. Such groups mobilize their actions over the Internet and are too varied, too complex, too otherworldly to enumerate here. But their presence has become ubiquitous and, for younger generations, essential.

We saw movements launched online. The "anti-globalization" movement really caught the public eye when it first began its interventions in multiple locations organizing its membership through the Internet. It was the absence of geographic boundaries that first characterized this community. But I am not sure what form anti-globalization activities can take now that such new horrific meaning has become attached to this discourse by acts of terrorism launched against the symbols of global capital. It is clear that, on one hand, the rapid move to globalization from business, industry, and governments will be difficult to turn back. The force propelling it forward, like the profit margin, for many is great. Yet there is an increasing concern about who is being excluded from the new "global village." Writing, thinking, and new discourses have been developed in an attempt to understand the impact on all aspects of society, from traditional indigenous communities to major urban centers.

A movement of young people, trying to bring conscience to this runaway train, became an international mobilization of resistance that used the vehicles of technology to convene, so to speak, its group meetings. And these protesters certainly kept the heads of state on alert in Seattle, Prague, Rome, and Genoa. However theatrical the actions of these groups are, and at times even futile their tactics may seem, they *are* deeply concerned with issues that, for the most part, do not affect them directly and are outside their local, personal spheres of interest. They are willing to travel great distances and put themselves at physical risk in order to communicate the injustices of global capitalism, and they are willing to assume that role until national leaders recognize such concerns and address them. The anti-globalization activists want to make apparent something many average citizens have already come to understand: "Our dependencies are now truly global, our actions, however, are, as before, local."[11] And for some it is precisely the local that is being affected by globalization, economically and culturally, leaving people impoverished on both fronts.

These activists are articulating universal fears about a world both exploding in complexity and speed of ideological change and shrinking in its intricate interconnectedness. These fears were manifested through the catastrophes in New York and Washington. Not only were those metropolitan centers deeply wounded by the events of September 11, the economies of places as far-flung as Hawaii, Switzerland, and Japan were affected as well. The acts of destruction were targeted at high finance and government, but they affected thousands of small businesses, factory workers, city workers, and artists, tumbling everyone into an already looming economic recession. No events could have been more local and yet, in cause and effect, more global.

When the buildup for the Iraq war began, demonstrations took place across the country, and thousands turned out for these marches. Many of those mobilizing the protestors were high school students who had not participated in such dramatic gestures before. Yet it was their energy—certainly this was true in Chicago—that motivated veterans of earlier protests to get back out on to the streets. Groups came together for that purpose as they always have, but this time word of mouth was a conversation in cyberspace. Many chat rooms and Web sites are in themselves manifestations of ethical communities, where those who share the same values, to keep difficult conversations alive, and those who protest injustice and reckless behavior, wherever they can, come together to share information, debate, and organize petitions, demonstrations, actions.

Where the Green Ants Dream

How can we reconcile contradictory claims of community—the premodern and the contemporary, the public and private spheres, the creative and reactionary, the local and the global? How can we truly measure the transformations of consciousness that occur every day, as people recognize, and begin to take responsibility for, their effect on this planet? I turn here to the work of an artist whose manifested vision of the intersection of incongruous meetings of cultural difference at times has allowed such contraries to coexist.

Werner Herzog's 1985 film *Where the Green Ants Dream* is in part about such extreme polarizations of lifestyles and values. Central to the plot is a confrontation between a group of aboriginal Australians and mining representatives who plan a series of explosions that they hope will yield valuable minerals. A young engineer chooses the site of demolition based on the richness of the ore to be found there. He is about to detonate the explosives when a group of aboriginal elders arrives to protect this site from violation.

We can easily imagine what happens next: The Australian aborigines, centered on a connection to the land, indigenous communities, ancient wisdom, and dreaming, stand in direct opposition to the mining company, which is run according to capitalist principles that affirm profit and the illusion of "progress" as the motivators of action and the annihilators of all ethical criteria. For the aborigines the situation is dire. They believe this is sacred land, where, at this precise location, the green ants are dreaming the universe into existence. If the ants are awakened, or the coherence of their dream disturbed, chaos might be unleashed and the planet obliterated.

What is apparent throughout the film is that speed is the most destructive force. The strength of the aborigines rests in their patience. They stop the project by slowing it down—sitting, chanting, and praying while refusing to move. They inform the young geologist that they represent 40,000 years on earth, and during that time they have not destroyed the land as the white man—a relative newcomer—has already done. Understanding the earth as they do, they have time on their side. They move slowly, refusing to be rushed. And the explosions are finally halted. The young geologist, deeply affected by the clarity and complexity of their vision and their power to actualize it, drops out of the center of modern life to join them on its peripheries. The aborigines not only win the battle but win over his consciousness as well.

Placing a high value on dreams and dreaming has been central to many aboriginal societies. We know this from studying indigenous American cultures like the Oglala Sioux, for whom dreams dreamt by holy men were taken so seriously that at times they were enacted by the entire tribe. We know that in indigenous cultures what is seen in dreams often becomes conscious subject matter for art and music. But in U.S. society, one of the most utilitarian of all societies, little value is placed on dreams and dreaming. We seem unwilling to affirm the integration of myth and the unconscious with consciousness and of our need for this to occur.

Dreaming for the future, Pierre Bourdieu tells us, is not likely to occur in "people who lack a hold on their present."[12] And certainly this characterizes contemporary U.S. society in general. But there are people, even now, who are constantly reimagining not just their future but also their present, and the present and future of the collective. They are the creative minds to which one must turn at times like these, when the world is sent into turmoil and the failure of a coherent vision for our own society's future is all too apparent. They are the green ants dreaming. They make the "art," as Bauman writes, "that transforms the improbable into the inevitable."[13] And they create innovative structures that help humanity.

If such values were central to the prevailing contemporary U.S. society, those who make their life's work the dreaming of the future of the society, not for their own economic aggrandizement but for humanity, would become its most valued citizens. Such creative people dream their dreams for the future on many fronts and can be found working in health care, education, numerous nongovernment offices, environmental agencies, urban planning, and in their studios as artists, designers, and intellectuals. The work of *dreaming the future* is at the core of the lives of such people and of such communities. Creative activist organizations are not only *against* but also *for*, no longer solely convened by place but also by ideas. Such communities, Slavoj Žižek suggests, can help us move from a society that says, as many citizens did in response to September 11, "A thing like this should not happen HERE!" to "A thing like this should not happen ANYWHERE!"[14] Such a simple shift could change America's approach to its own citizens, its foreign policy, and to the world.

It may be that globalization *is* truly the "revenge of the nomads,"[15] and movement has won out over staying put to redefine for many the notion of community as no longer only local and particular but global and inclusive. And it may be that the positive radicalness of this is that the hierarchies previously created to maintain oppressive forms of order will be transformed. But without a vision for how to use this potentially positive "disorder," new boundaries *will* be created along new lines. We have been watching such polarizing discourses enter the language every day since September 11. Without a sense of history, without a re-cognition of what has come before, new divisive patterns and hierarchies will simply replace the old. If we have learned anything from watching the destruction of the World Trade Center it is that the notion of progress is contested territory. One community's definition of progress is another's nightmare and target for destruction. Progress, as we have understood it in the West, *can be obliterated. Its dominance is not inevitable.*

Although it is fashionable to assume that in this century communities will become predominantly exterritorial, nongeographic, nonphysical, and that *place* itself will be irrevocably "devalued,"[16] there is still no doubt that what many crave is something as traditional, local, and essential to democracy as the Athenian agora, the public-market space, where ideas as well as goods are exchanged. The impetus for such space, whether actual or cyber, is to create a location where humans can meet as citizens to do the business of society, enjoy the company of others, and imagine engaging the process of the future together. Such places are also where humans can come together to mourn collective tragedy—another form of community—that turned a city as urban and urbane as New York into a village, where a local newspaper, the *New York Times*, told the stories and showed the faces of all who died on September 11. One hopes that by now all Americans recognize that, just as innocent people were killed in New York, innocent people have also died in Afghanistan, Iraq, and Pakistan, and that we are now deeply connected to these tragedies and will continue to be for decades.

Without recognizing how potentially powerful these desires for an ethical and humane response to the needs of others are—through activist projects, and acts of compassion, in physical space as well as in ideas—all visions of future communities will not satisfy, because they will deny the original community, the one we all share and, like all organic communities, rarely discuss—our humanity. The collective project of our species is to engage in its own conscious evolution beyond individual identity, difference, and nationhood. Its success can best be measured by how well we care for, protect, and value one another's lives. Such basic aspects of community take place in the tenth world of the most present present and should exist at the core of our species nature.

Notes

An earlier version of this chapter was presented in the paper series of the Andy Warhol Foundation for the Visual Arts (2002).

1. Zygmunt Bauman, *Community: Seeking Safety in an Insecure World* (Cambridge, UK: Polity Press, 2000), 12.

2. Ibid., 72.

3. Sigmund Freud, *Civilization and Its Discontents*, trans. Joan Riviere (New York: Doubleday Anchor, 1958).

4. Zygmunt Bauman, *The Individualized Society* (Malden, MA: Polity Press, 2001), 107.

5. Ibid.

6. Ibid., 106.

7. Bauman, *Community*, 13–14.

8. As cited in Bauman, *The Individualized Society*, 151.

9. As cited in ibid.

10. Ibid.

11. Ibid.

12. As cited in ibid., 29.

13. Ibid., 32.

14. Slavoj Žižek, "Welcome to the Desert of the Real," circulated on the Internet, November 2001: www.theglobalsite.ac.uk/times.

15. Bauman, *The Individualized Society*, 35.

16. Ibid., 38.

6
Pilgrimage to My Lai

⤙⤚

Vietnam the War never ends. It lurks in the shadows of U.S. history and emerges at difficult moments to stir up a past thick with denial.

The Stain

On March 16, 1968, the men of the eleventh brigade entered the village of My Lai, which they called Pinkville, and brutally murdered 504 Vietnamese civilians in a period of four hours. This "search and destroy" mission (General William Westmoreland's strategy of "flushing out" the Vietcong from their countryside "safe havens") soon transformed into a bloody massacre: "The killings took place, part maniacally, part methodically, over a period of about four hours," write Michael Bilton and Kevin Sim in *Four Hours in My Lai*, their chilling account of what happened on that day.[1] Several women were gang raped and killed with unconscionable brutality. Infants were blasted with machine-gun fire. The troops, whose average age was just twenty, were known as Charlie Company. They were under the leadership of Lieutenant William Calley—a name that has become synonymous with the nightmare of the war. He took his orders from Captain Ernest Medina, who received his commands from even higher up; those names still have not been spoken.

Lieutenant Calley was said to have forced a group of 100 to 170 villagers into a ditch and, without hesitation, slaughtered them all himself. Because of the nature of the war and the U.S. army's philosophy of killing "Vietcong in such large numbers that they could not be replaced,"[2] because of the pressure on unit commanders to produce enemy corpses, because it was so difficult for U.S. soldiers to "see the enemy" waging this guerrilla war, and because U.S. soldiers were being blown up constantly by land mines planted by this unseen enemy, "It is not surprising that some men acquired a contempt for human life and a predilection for taking it," observe Bilton and Sim. "In this sense," they continue, "My Lai was not an aberration of the war, but its apotheosis."[3]

This event was one of the turning points in U.S. citizens' perceptions of the extreme brutality of the war. American soldiers had entered an unarmed village firing, killing everyone and everything alive: Women, old men, children, babies, and animals. They then torched each house and all the vegetation surrounding the village. Although it was clear within minutes of the attack that there were no Vietcong in the village, that no one was armed and no one was returning fire, U.S. soldiers, having been told it was a Vietcong stronghold and that they were "to destroy everything in sight," did not desist from that directive. "It was worse than a massacre," write Bilton and Sim. "Too many of Medina's men were taking sordid pleasure in sadistic behavior."[4] It was this added realization that deeply disturbed all who heard about the massacre.

In fact, it was only because soldiers had been bragging about what had occurred in My Lai for almost a year that GI Ron Ridenhour, twenty-one years old, even heard about the massacre. He wrote letters to representatives in Congress, telling them that something awful and "bloody" had occurred. As a result of his insistence, a serious investigation took place. A U.S. army photographer, Sergeant Ronald Haeberle, who documented the massacre, was also key to this investigation. His photographs were used to substantiate the claim that only civilians had been murdered and in the most brutal ways. The following is an account given by a GI to investigators.

> An old papa-san was found hiding. His pants kept coming off. Two GIs dragged him out to be questioned. He was trying to keep his pants on. Captain Medina was doing the questioning. The old man didn't know anything. He rattled something off. Somebody asked Captain Medina what to do with the man, and Jay Roberts heard the captain say, "I don't care." Captain Medina walked away and Roberts heard a shot; the old man was dead.[5]

Sergeant Ronald Haeberle presented this account: "I remember ... two small children, one boy and one girl, kept walking toward us on this trail. They just kept walking toward us, you know, very nervously, very afraid, and you could hear the little girl saying, 'No, no,' in the Vietnamese tongue.... All of a sudden, the GIs just opened up and cut them down."[6] Sergeant Haeberle also recalled this incident:

> Off to the right a woman's form, a head, appeared from some brush. All the other GIs started firing at her, aiming at her, firing at her over and over again.

She had slumped over into one of those things that stick out of the rice paddies so that her head was a propped-up target. There was no attempt to question her or anything. They just kept shooting at her. You could see the bones flying in the air chip by chip.[7]

And the BBC reported the following: "Women were gang raped; Vietnamese who had bowed to greet the Americans were beaten with fists and tortured, clubbed with rifle butts, and stabbed with bayonets. Some victims were mutilated with the signature 'C Company' carved into the chest."[8]

The men who participated in these brutalities had lost many fellow soldiers in the recent Tet Offensive—the massive attacks on cities throughout South Vietnam that took place at the time of *Tet*—the lunar New Year in Vietnam. They had been told there *would* be Vietcong in the village, that it would be "hot," and they could get their revenge. Somewhere in all this lunacy these men lost their humanity and became rogue animals out for the kill. To them the Vietnamese were not civilians. They were not even human. Even babies were no exception; all were simply "the enemy."

In the midst of this frenzy of objectification and revenge, however, there were some men who simply refused to participate. They saw what was happening and condemned it. Among them was Herbert Carter, an African-American soldier who shot himself in the foot; it is assumed he did so because he did not want to take part in the massacre. There were helicopter pilot Hugh Thompson, Jr., door gunner Lawrence Colburn, and crew chief Glenn Adreotta, who landed their helicopter between rampaging American troops and the people of My Lai village. Thompson literally stood between the American troops and the bunker, shielding Vietnamese civilians with his body. He told his men in the helicopter, "If any of the Americans open up on the Vietnamese, we should open up on the Americans."[9] Thirty years later, two of these men received the Soldier's Medal from the U.S. government.

The American people did not know about the massacre at My Lai when it actually occurred. A year and a half later, discharged GIs who refused to let the story go brought it to the attention of the military, as well as to writers and journalists. In November 1969 Seymour M. Hersh wrote a piece called "Hamlet Attack Called Point-Blank Murder" in which he quoted a sergeant: "A few days before the mission, the men's general contempt for Vietnamese civilians intensified when some GIs walked into a landmine, injuring nearly 20 and killing at least one member of the company."[10]

There is no doubt that once the horror of My Lai was understood outside the military, it changed the course of the war. Innocent Vietnamese civilians were dying. American soldiers were dying. And many of the American soldiers who were still living had become sadistic and monstrous. It was clear that the American people had been misled by their government and did not know the level of brutality that was occurring daily. But once those outside the military were informed, many could not in good conscience allow the war to continue. The specific horrors of My Lai helped strengthen a growing consciousness that the war simply had to end.

Thirty-Four Years Later: Going to My Lai

After my first visit to Vietnam in 1996, I knew I would return with students. The thought of visiting the sites of the war and examining America's complex historical relationship to this country, as well as the possibility of exploring the many anthropological and art museums in the major cities and the wealth of Buddhist art throughout Vietnam, was too great a pedagogical opportunity not to pursue.

I did return in January 2002, with other faculty members—filmmaker Jeffrey Skoller and art historian Stanley Murashige—and ten students. We organized many expeditions during this trip together, but perhaps the most significant to many of us was the journey to My Lai. This chapter is my response to that experience.

As faculty, our basic intention for the trip was to take students who may have had only a vague understanding of what occurred in Vietnam and afford them an experience of the war and the country through the specificity of site. We hoped such explorations would, by analogy, translate into contemporary situations and help the students gain awareness of the historical and ongoing contradictions of American foreign policy. Within the context of the daily bombing of Afghanistan, often resulting in civilian casualties documented by the media, U.S. foreign policy was once again deeply in question.

The students who accompanied us were a mixture of undergraduate and graduate. Most, then in their twenties, had not even been born when the war took place, yet each of them felt drawn to Vietnam and wanted to move from thinking of Vietnam as a war to understanding it as a country. They were adventurers. Some had already traveled to distant places, others had never left the United States. None had been to Southeast Asia. Joining us as our research assistant was Vu Thu, a young artist I had met on my first visit to Hanoi. She subsequently came to the School of the Art Institute of Chicago as a postbaccalaureate student and was then accepted into the master's program in painting. For her, the trip had a different meaning: She was going home.

By traveling with us, she was choosing to encounter Vietnam through the eyes of Americans, some still filled with guilt for themselves and their country. Although many Vietnamese do not want to dwell on the past, many Americans of my generation still suffer the pain of what happened during the war. When I told a Vietnamese woman in a shop in Hoi An that we had visited My Lai, she said, "Don't feel bad about what you saw. We know it was your government and not you."

Like most of the students, Vu Thu was born right after the war ended, although her experience, of course, had been extraordinarily different from those of our other students. Her early years were steeped in poverty, reflecting the struggle of her parents and her country to recover economically. She had never traveled to the places we were going, and she had never even been to Ho Chi Minh City—the former Saigon. For her, the trip was a revelation. She was experiencing the totality of her country for the first time. And because she was willing to see Vietnam through our eyes, we had an opportunity to see it through hers.

Our goal was to visit many of the places whose names became well known to Americans during the war. We wanted to experience those places ourselves—to connect with what remains of the past in the present and to gain an understanding of what happened at those sites. In this spirit we visited Hanoi and Ho Chi Minh City. We boated down the Mekong River. We stopped at the DMZ (Demilitarized Zone) and drove to Khe Sahn and the coast of China Beach. We passed through Danang. We stayed in Hue. And of course we made a pilgrimage to My Lai, known to the Vietnamese now as Son My (pronounced *shun me*).

Of all the sites we visited over our three-week journey, no other had the psychological and emotional impact of My Lai. We absorbed the nightmare that had occurred there and left transformed. Without thinking too much about the weightiness of the term, some of us began to call the visit to My Lai a "pilgrimage," probably choosing this word because of our awareness that we wanted to know the place not just through the mind but more deeply, in the body. This is the type of secular experience many of us associated with pilgrimage and, in such thinking, we were not alone.

Freud Visits the Acropolis

Although we generally associate pilgrimage with a deeply religious notion of transformation through peripatetic movement, many pilgrimages induce unique effects—the result of physically going to a place of symbolic meaning.

In 1936, late in his life, Sigmund Freud wrote an essay called "A Disturbance of Memory on the Acropolis."[11] It was a tribute to writer Romain Rolland on Rolland's seventieth birthday. The essay recounts a trip Freud made with his brother to Athens some thirty years before and the multifarious meanings he extracted from that journey.

The essay begins with this narrative: Presented with the possibility of visiting Athens, Freud becomes both depressed and anxious. Although he has always wanted to visit the Acropolis, has always dreamed of what it would be like, for complex and remarkably predictable neurotic reasons (such as not wanting to usurp his father), Freud cannot believe that he might actually have the opportunity to do so. When he finally makes the journey, a series of unexpected emotions dominates his response. But most significant in the context of our visit to My Lai, Freud realizes, once at the site, that he never fully believed the Acropolis existed, that it was in fact *there,* or *anywhere.*

"If I may make a slight exaggeration," Freud writes, "it was as if someone, walking beside Loch Ness, suddenly caught sight of the form of the famous Monster stranded upon the shore and found himself driven to the admission: So it really *does* exist—the sea-serpent we've never believed in!"[12] The fact of the "occurrence of this idea on the Acropolis" had precisely shown Freud that in his unconscious he "had *not* believed in it." Only by *going* did he come to understand, as he says, that he could acquire a "conviction" in its existence that "reached down to the unconscious."[13]

At first his conscious and unconscious minds could not come together in an integrative fashion to accept the reality of place, even though he stood on the physical site and understood, at least in his mind, that he was at the most luminous place of antiquity—the sacred rock where one went to worship the gods, the *Acro-polis*—the place *above the city.*

Such feelings of dissociation often accompany our arrival at a much-anticipated place or experience of a long-awaited event, giving the sensation that we are not "all there," or that what is taking place is not "really happening." At more devastating moments, when consciousness splits and we cannot accept the reality of what has occurred, this can lead to a sense of living in a bad dream from which one soon will awaken. Depression and anxiety result when one realizes that there is no awakening *from,* no place to awaken *to,* for one is already awake.

Another form of surprising dissociation can occur when what happens is, as we say, "too good to be true." Something we never imagined occurs. Because we are in disbelief that such a thing could happen to us, we assume it cannot be true. This occurrence may simulate a pleasant dream, but we might think it cannot possibly be *our* dream. Or if it is our dream, then we will soon awaken. This explains why we often fail to experience the best moments of our lives. The multiple bodies of consciousness are unable to completely internalize the event.

Traveling to places of great symbolic significance can embody all this complexity and more. One goes to know the place in the physical body, to have an experience of the place, and then to have that experience recorded somewhere in the body, so it then can be accessed as memory by the mind and the spirit. Such journeys are performative rituals. The *going to* and the *being there* require preparation and are dependent on the body for completion of the experience.

Perhaps this is why we called our journey to My Lai a pilgrimage. For those of us who lived through the Vietnam War, even the name sent a sick reverberation through the cells of our bodies. For the younger generation, there was a great deal to learn about the event before they could feel the impact of the name, the place, and the trauma that had occurred there. But by the end of the journey, we were all equally turned inside ourselves, creating a type of silence that occurs when humans struggle, in their bodies, to absorb an excess of pain.

The Nature of Pilgrimage

Various conditions are associated with the notion of pilgrimage. The most primary is the simple movement away from and toward place. Peter Harbison, in *Pilgrimage in Ireland,* writes: "What sparked the first Christian pilgrimage was the desire felt by St. Paul to stand on the same ground the Savior had trodden."[14]

One needs to leave the mundanity of one's life and become a seeker of that which is sacred—in oneself, in the world, and in those metaphysical realms that cannot be known in this world. In order to set out on a pilgrimage, space must metamorphose into metaphor. Once the journey has begun, the ground one walks on and the distance one travels become a mirror for the evolution of one's own spirituality. This is an important element of pilgrimage—while walking, journeying, traveling to a designated place, the act of getting there becomes as important as the arrival. During that time of travel, it is assumed that one will undergo a certain transformation of consciousness that cannot be achieved when one is immersed in daily life. Harbison continues, "The act of going on pilgrimage is common to many religions, not only Christianity but Islam, Hinduism, and Buddhism as well. Nomadic people feel no need for it, as they are on the move anyway. It is a phenomenon found only among settled communities, usually those which have a considerable cultural development behind them."[15]

The act of going on pilgrimage may derive from a desire to seek absolution, but it might also be an expression of pain and compassion. It might come from needing or wanting something for oneself or one's loved ones, or, as in the case of our visit to My Lai, it might be a symbolic gesture, not only for oneself, but also for one's country—an attempt to resolve what remains unresolved. Whatever the motivation, there is a purposefulness about such a journey that separates it from the randomness and pleasure seeking of mundane travel. The intention of this type of journey is not to change the world, but to change oneself—to achieve a consciousness and spiritual transformation while connecting with the history of others who have trodden the same path.

The time of the journey (which for the pilgrims of the Middle Ages might have extended over years) becomes mythic. It moves us into another, more informal way of measuring time that is much more internal and upon which one places a great deal of symbolic meaning. If this meaning is shared by a large group of people, as it often is when connected to famous sites of pilgrimage—such as Croagh Patrick in Ireland or Santiago de Compostela in Spain—then the journey takes place in mythic time and mythic space. In *Roads to Santiago,* Cees Nooteboom writes:

> It is impossible to prove and yet I believe it: there are some places in the world where one is mysteriously magnified on arrival or departure by the emotions of all those who have arrived and departed before....
>
> At the entrance of the cathedral in Santiago de Compostela there is a marble column with deep impressions of fingers, an emotional, expressionistic claw created by millions of hands ... by laying my hand in the hollow one I was participating in a collective work of art. An idea becomes visible in matter.... The power of an idea impelled kings, peasants, monks to lay their hands on exactly that spot on the column, each successive hand removed the minutest particle of marble so that, precisely where the marble had been erased, a negative hand became visible.[16]

This is the symbolic made manifest through gesture. You can only participate in this collective act by physically standing in the exact place others have stood—St. Paul's motivation to stand where Christ had walked or going to the exact spot where the Buddha was first enlightened.

One can speak of sites that have seen pilgrims for centuries, like Santiago de Compostela, but one can also speak of places that have become sacred overnight, like the former World Trade Center. At first the World Trade Center site was a place of horrific devastation, but it quickly became a place of visitation and mourning for New Yorkers, and then for those who traveled to the city. There has been a viewing platform from which people could observe the location of the buildings' collapse. There is no longer anything physical to witness. Nonetheless, people come to pay homage and to see with their own eyes, to feel in their own bodies the tremendous emptiness that remains. The site will always be considered hallowed ground memorializing the thousands who died there.

The authors of *Image and Pilgrimage in Christian Culture* write, "a tourist is half a pilgrim, if a pilgrim is half a tourist."[17] We might say that one difference between pilgrims and tourists is that for pilgrims, the road *to* the site, the process of getting there, is as important as the arrival. It is filled with the anticipation of some spiritual event that will occur as they travel, when they arrive, and while they are there. This, of course, can be true of tourism as well: One can anticipate the Cathedral at Cologne, the Pyramids, or even the Acropolis as did Freud, with a sense that after having experienced these phenomena, one will never be the same. The difference is that a great deal of tourism is about consumption and acquisition of culture, the natural landscape, or both. One seeks out certain places because it is believed that to be a cultured or worldly person, one must have the experience of visiting them—Venice, Paris, Istanbul, the Grand Canyon, Niagara Falls, the Taj Mahal, the Nile. One visits just to have seen them, just to know, in a sense, what all the fuss is about. In this acquisitive mode, many will photograph, and some will physically take something from the site, such as stones from the foundation of the Parthenon, pieces of the Berlin Wall, magazine cutouts of movie stars from Anne Frank's bedroom walls in the Annex. Others would be horrified to remove anything from such sites and will want to alchemize the experience psychically.

Pilgrims journey for the spirit, seeking purification or the granting of a wish or a prayer, while most others who travel are attracted by the external phenomena they might encounter. Some even want to circumvent the *going* entirely. Years ago I was quite taken aback when my mother suggested, only a bit tongue-in-cheek, that my trip to Bellagio, Italy, could have been avoided had I simply visited the Bellagio in Las Vegas. "You don't really need to travel anymore. You have it all in Las Vegas," she said. Some will be satisfied with simulacra. Others will always have to go.

But why? What does one want from such experiences? For those who have studied art history, the thought of seeing the actual paintings of Fra Angelico in Florence in the cells and niches of the Dominican priory for which they were painted is comparable to a religious experience, not because of the content of the paintings per se, but because one is transformed by what Walter Benjamin refers to as "aura," the experience of the art, as it was meant to be had in its intended actual location. No matter how many replicas of the Acropolis we might find in Nashville, Tennessee, there is nothing like standing on the actual site. The air, the light, the position of the rock over the city embracing its totality from 360 degrees, and its arched posture looking down at the agora, the place in which it has stood since antiquity, are transformative. The experience links the traveler, pilgrim, and tourist with history and, in this case, with the evolution of Western civilization. It makes the past present, transforms the present into the past. Walking up to the Acropolis or down from it, one imagines that the cicadas one hears have been there for centuries. Nothing you can read, no simulations you may see, can give you that sensation. And why is that? Because the experience takes place only through the flesh. It is the *physical knowing* that links us to the body of collective memory.

There is a moveable wall called *The Wall That Heals* that simulates the permanent Vietnam Veterans Memorial designed by Maya Lin. The portable wall, which is a half-scale replica made of powder-coated aluminum, can never embody the physical and spiritual gravity of the actual granite wall. It has not absorbed the pain of the millions who have come to the actual wall as mourners and supplicants for decades now, praying on behalf of those who died. And although many viewers find the portable wall powerful, it cannot hold the weight of the 58,000 Americans and all the Vietnamese who died or the faith in the United States that died for many with the pain and shame that accompanied the war. At the actual wall in Washington, D.C., one doesn't even need to see the wall to feel its presence. Walking toward it, one begins to internalize the palpable sadness of the thousands who have come before. The memorial has become a repository for all the complex emotions associated with the war. For many Vietnam veterans it has become a destination for pilgrimage.

Such space is the opposite of non-space, mall-space, suburban space, corporate, generic, or interchangeable space—the spaces of postmodernity. And it is the opposite of cyberspace, the place of post-postmodernism. The Vietnam Veterans Memorial is a well-designed and conceptualized space that has become ritualized through the spontaneity of the masses. As the artist and architect of this project, Maya Lin could never have imagined how her design would be transformed.

The Vietnam Veterans Memorial was also immediately turned into a site of offering by all the visitors who brought things to it and left them behind. A museum will house the collection of objects left at the wall. Similarly, handmade altars immediately marked the perimeter of Ground Zero in New York, and candles, flowers, photos, offerings were left at the site.

Pilgrimages have always been democratic in just this way. For the Greeks, the long journey to Delphi was about locating the future, the travel to Eleusis about finding the Mysteries—the fate that would befall them after death. In Christianity such pilgrimages existed outside the hierarchy of the church and the domain of priests and clerics. They arose spontaneously. Their perpetuation built community. Seekers of all kinds became equals as they undertook the journey. Because every pilgrim who comes must walk up the very difficult mountain of shale to get to the top of Croagh Patrick, the journey becomes about the community that is formed each time by those making it. They all find, in turn, their own internal peace through the process. Historically, when seekers could not physically go on such journeys, there were simulated pilgrimages close to home, such as that designed for the cathedral of Chartres. One could walk the length of the pilgrimage "in time" in the cathedral's eleven-circuit stone labyrinth set in the nave. This could serve as a substitute for the actual pilgrimage to Jerusalem and as a result came to be known as *Chemin de Jerusalem* (Road to Jerusalem). But in the actual journeys, the going is far different from the return, or, as Victor and Edith Turner write: "Indeed, even when pilgrims return by the way they came, the total journey may still be represented, not unfittingly, by an ellipse, if psychological factors are taken into account. For the return road is, psychologically, different from the approach road."[18] The purposefulness and focus of the *going* may be over, while the *returning* to one's own life is full of a new expectation—that one will somehow return transformed.

Why Did We Go? What Did We Find?

On the bus from Hue to My Song (Me Shun), the district in which My Lai is located, we were, as usual, rather active and boisterous—asking our guide where he was during the years of the American war, as the Vietnamese call it, how his life had been during that time. Students were talking to each other, writing in their journals, listening to music, cramming in as much information as they could about the place we were about to visit. Engaged with the magnificence of the landscape, faculty and students alike were also photographing or filming out the windows. But the road back, although physically the same (there is only one north-south route through Vietnam), was not the road previously traveled. On the journey back, there was silence.

What did we find at My Lai? Everything and nothing. Nothing, of course, remains of the village. There are now only headstones where houses once stood. Engraved into each are the names of those who died. The engraving might say, "Foundation of Mr. Phon Cong's house burnt by U.S. soldiers; four of his family members were murdered: Phan Hong, 65; Le Thi Duoc, 36; Phan San, 12; Phan Thi Tranh, 6," or the following: "Foundation of Mr. Nguyen Cai's house burnt by U.S. soldiers. Three of his family members were murdered: Phung Thi Hiep, 31; Nguyen Thi Hwe, 12; Nguyen Thi Be, 3."

The now-overgrown ditch at My Lai. *Photograph by Carol Becker.*

These were the people in the village when the Americans arrived—mothers, children, grandparents. At each stone where there was once a house there is now a place to burn incense for the dead, provided for us at the entrance to the site. There is also the ditch, now overgrown with plants, but still unmistakable as the site into which between 100 and 170 people were pushed and then shot. Jasmine and hibiscus have overgrown this site, which is now as green and resplendent as the rest of the Vietnamese countryside.

There is one stucco structure, and in this building are large black-and-white and color photographs, very specific, about the massacre. After looking at several and reading the captions that appear next to them in Vietnamese and English, one realizes that for these photos to exist at all, someone had to be watching the massacre while it was occurring and, more astoundingly, documenting it. Then you read the text: The photographer taking the pictures was Ronald Haeberle, the official U.S. army photographer assigned to that platoon on that day. The images taken for the army and those he took with his own camera for himself became important evidence in the investigation to prove that a massacre had actually occurred. After the war, a set of prints was given to the Vietnamese government. They comprise a great deal of the material in the memorial museum.

The documentation allows us to walk through the massacre moment by moment—people being rounded up, terror on their faces. Children crying, clutching at their mothers; very old bony men walking toward the camera with their arms in the air in gestures of surrender. Piles of bodies in the ditch, one thrown over the other randomly, reminiscent of the mounds of human remains found at Bergen-Belsen, Germany, after the camps were liberated in 1945. In the midst of this bedlam are photos of Lieutenant Thompson with a special declaration to his bravery and humanity. Although he was only able to save one life, his gesture of refusal has earned him heroic status in Vietnam.

Taking up an entire wall is a list of all those who died: 504 names, with their ages at death. The long list is reminiscent of Maya Lin's wall of the dead, which is categorized by date. The Vietnamese have organized those killed during the massacre in family clusters: The oldest in each family is listed first; the children are always last. This wall became the focal point for a performance created by two students on our return.

Transubstantiation

Perhaps it was the humility and lushness of the place, its green serenity. Or that we had traveled so far to get to it and then back to Hoi An that night, allowing time for contemplation. Or it was that this part of the journey was focused on one horrific incident in one annihilated village. Or it was because we had a very specific purpose in going there—to stand on the ground where the massacre had occurred and to pay homage to those who died. Through the particularity, perhaps we could almost imagine the magnitude of the totality.

We did not go to My Lai to judge. The verdict on that event was determined long ago. As Hannah Arendt said, in an interview given to Günter Grass in 1964, in reference to the death camps in Germany: "*This ought not to have happened*. Something happened there, to which we cannot reconcile ourselves. None of us ever can."[19] My Lai, once a village, now a memorial, was determined to have been the site of a massacre by 1970. Lieutenant Calley was sentenced to life in prison, but this sentence was soon commuted, and he actually only served four and a half years in a very well-protected and comfortable prison. After this he ran his father-in-law's jewelry shop in Columbus, Georgia, where he drove a Mercedes-Benz given to him by a supporter and hid from reporters and others asking about the war.

Among less fortunate Vietnam veterans there have been many suicides, murders, and men incapacitated for civilian life whose tragic situations are traced to their involvement in My Lai. "The massacre had become a matter for individual conscience alone," write Bilton and Sim.[20] Those who set the policies and gave the orders, and the country that engaged in this war, have retained their psychic freedom, while those who followed the orders laid out by others, and were thus driven to horrific acts, live under a weight of guilt they cannot abide. Some of these individuals continue to suffer for their actions every day and will do so for the rest of their lives.

In 1977 the ten-year-old son of Vietnam veteran Varnardo Simpson was killed while playing in his front yard. Teenagers across the road began arguing. One pulled out a gun and a wild shot inadvertently hit the boy in the head. Varnardo Simpson will never recover. For him, his son's death marks his punishment for brutally killing twenty-five people in My Lai when he was twenty-five years old. Paranoid, he no longer leaves his house. As Bilton and Sim say, for Simpson, "Remembering has become a compulsion."[21]

These authors understand such men to be scapegoats in the Old Testament sense. They are like the "chosen goat"

> who, having had laid upon his head all the sins and transgressions of the Children of Israel, was then led by a fit man "unto a land not inhabited." These original scapegoats did not merely take the blame for the sins of others; they were machines for forgetting, for transporting as far away as possible, out of sight and out of mind, the sins of the entire community. Only after they had bathed their flesh and washed their clothes were the men who led the scapegoats into the wilderness allowed back to camp. For the scapegoats themselves, however, there was no return.[22]

By journeying to such a place as My Lai, it was our hope to develop our own form of absolution. Bilton and Sim write, "National Consciousness consists of what is allowed to be forgotten as much as by what is remembered."[23] The philosopher Giorgio Agamben writes: "Human beings are human in so far as they bear witness to the inhuman."[24] We came to bear witness through remembering and reclaiming memory across generations. I was as young as some of our students when I first had to take responsibility for my relationship to the war: Had I been male, would I have gone? As a female, what actions might I take to stop the war? How much was I willing to risk?

The silence on the bus on our return journey was our way of absorbing into our individual psyches what can hardly ever be absorbed—and that is tragedy—the chaos generated through human volition that can be given shape and structure only by the writing of history and the making of art, forms that provide temporary containment for the uncontainable and allow the unspeakable to be spoken without destroying either the speaker or the audience.

Why do artists and writers, in particular, need to go to the actual place of trauma? What is it they hope to find? A quality of light? Past images juxtaposed to contemporary life? Words used to describe an event that will trigger a reaction and allow them to assume their roles as custodians of memory? Agamben quotes the poet Friedrich Hölderlein's statement: "What remains is what the poets found.... The poetic word is the one that is always situated in the position of a remnant and that can therefore bear witness ... found language as what remains, as what actually survives the possibility, or impossibility, of speaking."[25]

If artists and writers are unique in their relationship to such journeys, it is that they are willing to bear witness and to do it by using such remnants to create an event or physical entity to mark their experience—a work of art, be it an essay, a poem, a film, a performance. However ephemeral, they will find a way to alchemize their internalization of the event into a further manifestation, filtered through the particularity of individual consciousness. In this way *their* work becomes interpretation, a gesture of remembering. Such responses—which often locate the humanity in the inhumanity—are as much about the person seeing as about the place being seen.

This is the transformative potential of art—its ability to take what is left of the incomprehensibility of human action and find a way to re-present it back into the collective; not to hide it or to hide from it, not to avoid the personal responsibility of collective action, but to allow the humanness in the inhumanity to be seen and its meaning made manifest. Such is the responsibility and challenge many of us feel, to keep alive that which some would like to see buried. We can only hope that we will all be so completely revolted by what we see that we will finally understand that war destroys not only its victims, but also its perpetrators.

When we returned from the trip two students—American-born Jessica Almy Pagan and Vietnamese-born Vu Thu—constructed a durational performance, at the core of which Thu teaches Jessica to repeat, in correct Vietnamese, every name on the list of the 504 civilians killed on that day. By the rules Jessica established, she can only move on to the next name when she has correctly pronounced the preceding one. Needless to say, this takes time. The names are the remnants, all that remains of those who died. Her struggle to learn these names and say them correctly allows her to bear witness to the lives they represent.

Jessica became absorbed by the history of My Lai and deeply motivated to make it the subject of her work when she realized that at the exact time the massacre was taking place, between 9:00 A.M. and 1:00 P.M. on the morning of March 16, 1968, across the world and the international date line, she was being born. This exercise became her way of acknowledging each life that was lost. Witnessing in such a way allowed her to establish a relationship to each person who was killed that day. Perhaps she chose such literal speech so as not to be completely silent and to inhabit that space Agamben describes for such testimony, a liminal zone between the sayable and the unsayable. If My Lai causes silence, as an artist, Jessica has found a way to speak. She is one of the witnesses who are "neither the dead nor the survivors, neither the drowned nor the saved." She is, in Agamben's terms, "what remains between them."[26]

Such are the responses of those who travel to respond—pilgrims who come armed with cameras, tape recorders, and notebooks, all in preparation to reuse creatively the traumas of the past. Not to hide from them or to hide them from us, not to obscure, but to clarify knowledge by moving it through the body, allowing it to leave its mark on us, like that already drawn onto the history of the world, those circles carved into the inner trunk of a gigantic tree that record the tumultuousness of nature and the tree's struggle to survive each year. If we become adept at reading such marks and making them our own, we might say the following:

This was a year of much rain. This was a year of drought, and this was a year when something happened that we just cannot explain. All we know is that events etched an erratic, disturbed ellipse on the tree's core. Growth stopped for a time. Branches surely withered; some fell. With a mirror we can reverse the order of this knowledge and play it back. Our minds begin to reconstruct what occurred and absorb its meaning. We wish we could erase the mark, see it gone forever. But the inscription is indelible and at times inaudible—a silent, persistent stain. Taking the body of this history into our own, we transform it and, through those forms available to us, respond.

Notes

An earlier version of this chapter was published in *Art Journal* (Winter 2003).
1. Michael Bilton and Kevin Sim, *Four Hours in My Lai* (New York: Penguin Books, 1992), 3.

2. Ibid., 32.

3. Ibid., 14.

4. Ibid., 14.

5. Hal Wingo, "The Massacre at My Lai," *Life* 67, no. 23 (December 5, 1969), 36–45, taken from the Web site http://karws.gso.uri.edu/Marsh/Vietnam/mylait01. htm, 5.

6. Ibid.

7. Ibid., 2

8. "Murder in the Name of War—My Lai," BBC News Online, July 20, 1998. Available at news.bbc.co.uk/1/low/world/asia-pacific/64344.stm.

9. Hugh Thompson, Jr., was a helicopter reconnaissance pilot. This quote was taken from the wall of a small exhibit of "heroic" American figures presented by the Vietnamese at the site of the massacre.

10. Seymour M. Hersh, "Hamlet Attack Called Point-Blank Murder," in *Reporting Vietnam*, vol. 2 (New York: Library of America, 1998), 19.

11. Sigmund Freud, "A Disturbance of Memory on the Acropolis: An Open Letter to Romain Rolland on the Occasion of His Seventieth Birthday," *The Standard Edition of the Complete Psychological Works of Sigmund Freud*, trans. James Strachey, vol. 22 (London: Hogarth Press, 1986), 238–48.

12. Ibid., 241.

13. Ibid.

14. Peter Harbison, *Pilgrimage in Ireland: The Monuments and the People* (London: Rarrie and Jenkins, 1997), 23.

15. Ibid.

16. Cees Nooteboom, *Roads to Santiago: A Modern Day Pilgrimage through Spain*, trans. Ina Rilke (New York: Harcourt, 1997), 3.

17. Victor Turner and Edith Turner, *Image and Pilgrimage in Christian Culture: Anthropological Perspectives* (New York: Columbia University Press, 1978), 20.

18. Ibid., 32.

19. Cited in Giorgio Agamben, *Remnants of Auschwitz: The Witness and the Archive*, trans. Danielle Heller-Roazen (New York: Zone Books, 1999), 71.

20. Bilton and Sim, *Four Hours in My Lai*, 36.

21. Ibid., 7.

22. Ibid., 361.

23. Ibid., 4.

24. Agamben, *Remnants of Auschwitz*, 121.

25. Ibid., 161.

26. Ibid., 164.

7
Archives of Apartheid

⌐⊖

Dedicated to the memory of Florence N. Mdlolo, who died tragically as I was writing this essay.[1]

The Truth and Reconciliation's greatest contribution was to give back to South Africa its heart.[2]

At a press conference Mandela took De Klerk's hand and said, "We must forgive but never forget."[3]

Conceived by South African sculptor Andries Botha, the project *Amazwi Abesifazane*, Voices of Women, has been centered around the production of "memory cloths"—small embroidered, sometimes beaded pieces of colored fabric that tell the stories of traumatic events experienced by indigenous women, most of them Zulu and from the townships of South Africa.[4] These are the stories that have been left out of the discussions about the nightmares of apartheid. Involving more than two thousand participants, the project has attempted to create a forum so that these women might finally be heard while they cultivate their own creativity, earn money from such work, develop their consciousness as women, occupy their rightful place in history, and connect with other indigenous women globally.

The process begins with workshops in which women are encouraged to write (if they can), or to tell someone who then transcribes, a narrative about a traumatic event they witnessed or experienced directly during the years of apartheid—something they cannot forget. They are then encouraged to represent their stories visually. Many of these women have highly developed skills with thread or beads; others are embroidering for the first time. Each woman makes one cloth for exhibition or sale and one for the archive. Many of these cloths have been sold locally and internationally, encouraging the creativity of the woman involved and, in a small way, helping them to achieve their goal of economic independence. An exhibition of eighty such depictions, each mounted and framed with a photo of the woman and her written text, opened simultaneously with the Third World Conference Against Racism, Racial Discrimination, Xenophobia and Related Intolerance in Durban in 2001.

This project takes its impetus from the national endeavor to construct social memory. Since 1995 South Africa has attempted to make transparent, and then to reconcile, the thirty years of apartheid. The act of creating the Truth and Reconciliation Commission, and the years of public testimony, confession, and debate that followed, have changed South Africa. The new progressive constitution guarantees that it will never be possible for it to return to the fascist state it once was. Nor can it any longer hide the consequences of apartheid. It is into this environment of ongoing historical and psychological reflection and debate about the past and its implications for the future that *Amazwi Abesifazane* was imagined into being.

The project brings to this ongoing conversation about history and the construction of a national archive a focus on the often-undocumented lives of indigenous women, many of whom are from the rural areas and townships that suffered extreme violence. Writes poet and essayist Njabulo Ndebele:

> The homelands were another arena of gross violations of human rights. KwaZulu-Natal, the Ciskei, and KwaNdebele, in particular ... suffered cyclical attacks and counter-attacks in which the line between victims and perpetrators blurred as comrades and vigilantes assumed both roles. ... In the townships, people experienced "necklace killings," the burning of houses of suspected spies, and a reign of terror by groups acting in the name of liberation.[5]

These are the experiences that the women of *Amazwi Abesifazane* recorded. The "object of their labor" was to create a representation of social memory, written and visual, that can provide an important addition to the national archive—a collective indictment of apartheid's maleficence.

How does one remember what one most wants to forget? Why does one choose to remember at all? At the core of the project is the attempt to re-create history from memory and to conjure memory through narrative—written and imaged.

Each cloth is a bit of archival information. The act of telling brings another story filled with important historical and cultural data into the public arena and adds it to the now almost two thousand others. In so doing it links the history of the individual with that of other women in similar circumstances. It brings each woman into a process that is as much about the future as it is about the past. While women do this concentrated work of telling and stitching, they reflect. But it is in the sharing of the past that the patterns that affect all their lives become most apparent.

They begin to describe to one another how they have been treated within patriarchal structures, both by the systems of apartheid, invented and executed by white men, and also by systems of patriarchy within tribal structures that allow for the dominance of black men. In both, black women are at the bottom of the hierarchy, often sexually abused, abandoned, and economically exploited. Their children are at times murdered.

It is through the telling of the stories in words and images that women first begin to understand that their lives, their stories, and their positions within the narrative are similar to those of other women. Another goal is to link women to global movements that have developed in Latin America, Canada, and Africa. Hence, women who are often most excluded from conversations about globalization and its effects on their daily lives have created a forum within which to debate such issues.

The cloths give voice to these narratives, and from them we learn each individual woman's trauma but also the cumulative weight of trauma marked by repetition through the narratives of humiliation, brutality, and the sheer randomness of tragedy among people who have few allies and fewer options. It also becomes clear that it is these women who are the caretakers of the most at-risk members of society—children. All it takes is the loss of one caretaker to create an untenable situation for a child who can never be salvaged. Thabisile Dlamini writes:

> Granny died while sleeping on her bed and I loved her as she loved me. She was doing everything for me as my mother had died while I was young. After that I went to stay with my aunt, Zinhle (who was my uncle's wife), who abused me saying that she had no place for orphans and she was not even giving me food. She made me leave school and look after her children.... Even my uncle, Busani, does not care about anything. However, I am still staying with them and there is nothing I can do because they are my relatives.[6]

The rural world of South Africa was then, and still is, a very precarious place; a random act can lead to a tragedy from which an entire family might never recover. Fire is a good example. A fire may have been caused by someone setting a torch to a home during an instance of township violence, or it may have begun while someone was cooking under primitive conditions, or when a child raced through a space and overturned a lantern. But when there are no safety precautions to stop it, fire easily rages out of control. And like water during a flood, it takes with it the few possessions people have.

Under these conditions, once one loses a home, it is almost impossible to secure another. The family then usually splinters—children are sent to live with one relative, the mother to stay with another. Or the mother may be a domestic worker during the week, living at the home of a white family, while her mother takes care of her children in the township. But once the home is lost, the mother may never be able to live with her children again. The father may already be absent because of the nature of work under the apartheid system, where black miners might be gone for months at a time; or because of the fragmentation of the male psyche—the result of such ritualized separations; or just because of the omnipresent instability and humiliation bred under apartheid and the way it affected men.

In apartheid South Africa, blacks lived under a government that not only did not care about their welfare but actively sought to destabilize them by keeping the majority black population uneducated and powerless while fomenting township violence through a campaign of paranoia. Njabulo Ndebele comments on the Truth and Reconciliation Commission report: "It shows how communities of the oppressed, torn apart by fear, suspicion and mistrust, desperate to build and preserve unity, were led to hunt down people thought to be informers and collaborators. They met a gruesome fate."[7]

The narratives recorded through *Amazwi Abesifazane*, though brief, convey both subtle and overt abuses of power. The following stories give only the slightest glimpse of the breadth of daily life recorded in the project's archive.

In 1976 Murial Linda was a domestic worker for a white family. Of this experience she writes:

> They had a big dog, which I had to give food to every time I left. They usually gave me bread and tea. One day he gave me food which was left over from the previous day, as they had had a party. When I sat down and ate, I was very surprised to find out that the food was in a bowl that I had used to give food to the dog. When I asked him why he did that, he said that there was no problem because a bowl gets washed. He, too, could eat from it. I asked to be relieved of my duties. They all laughed.

Of life in Newlands in 1969, Mildred Mkhulise writes:

> Black people were being evicted from their land by whites who claimed they had bought that land; when black people produced some documents of their own to show that they had a right too to be on that land, that did not help. Police vans with bulldozers came. They had dogs with them. They were harshly evicted. Their belongings were thrown all over the place. My home, too, was destroyed in that way. When we came back from school my uncle was sitting like that with our belongings.

Elsie Nyembezi writes, "My father was working in Durban and when my stepmother went to the hospital to give birth, she left a message that I was going to leave school so that I would look after the baby and I did so but I was only in grade one. Even today I can't read and write and I don't forgive her because I can't get a job because she was abusing me. Her children, though, are well educated and they have good jobs."

Thandi Nyawose writes:

This was done by the warriors at Kwa-Mashu, section E. The warriors stabbed and killed six children in 1987. These children were coming back from school. These warriors claimed that these children had beaten up Shabalala's goat. They caught them first and put them into a *combi* (truck) and took them into the bush where they killed them. There was only one survivor. He is the one who told the whole story of what happened.

The stories, written in Zulu predominantly, have been translated, then archived, in both their original native language and in English. From the stories came the images. The complexity of the narrative is illustrated through stitches, design, and color. Some women have greater facility for either telling or sewing; some are adept at both. The stories are often filled with a great deal of movement—people running or being beaten by police, crowds chasing and then killing a suspected spy, fire raging through a village, cars colliding. Intricate weavings of red thread around the dirt-covered head of a battered man to signify blood, miniature representations of underwear left strewn around the naked body of a stick-figure woman who appears to have been violated. Sometimes the woman herself is represented in the cloth, or she might be telling the story of others— something she has witnessed and cannot forget. In certain cloths every inch is covered in details; in others the images are sparse, alluding only to key factors in the story.

The horror of the cloths often rests in the almost childlike representation of figures drawn by women who may have little training in representation, juxtaposed to the devastating astuteness with which they understand and recount brutality in its most overt and subtle manifestations. At times the images even seem innocent, benign, beautiful, or playful in form and color, until one reads the fragment of text and understands the actual meaning of, for example, a small, awkward male figure represented with a thick black ring encircling his chest. The story tells us that he is captured and about to be set alight through "necklacing"—the township practice of placing a suspected traitor in a public space, forcing an automobile tire around his (or her) neck, and then igniting it with kerosene.

All the women involved in the project have benefited enormously from such reflection on their lives. But for one woman in particular, the project

Florence N. Mdlolo. *Violence in 1996–97: Train Victims,* 2001–02. Cloth with embroidery and beadwork, 10.5" x 13.75", irreg.

provided a way in which to tell not just a bit of her story, but her entire story. Florence N. Mdlolo wrote her memoir and then illustrated each episode (forty in all) with its own memory cloth. Some of her stories, like all those told, seem unimaginably brutal, and yet they occurred. They at times reflect township conflicts between the ANC (African National Congress) and the IFP (Inkatha Freedom Party), which were very often fueled by the National Party—the governing party of apartheid. She writes:

(1996–1997) Violence victimized us all. Families starved as stores closed. They were fighting over taxi routes. People hid at the 17 cemetery yard to try and save their lives. They had lost their conscience that graves are to be respected. One would find them there feeding their babies when one had come to bury a relative. Sounds of gunfire would be heard sometimes while they were cooking. Those who had a chance would run away with the food. Some were sleeping on top of the graves. The violence continued for three years.

Florence N. Mdlolo also tells stories of helplessness in the face of natural disaster in remote locations:

Many children had been in the fields watching the newly seeded sorghum to keep the birds from eating the seeds. It started raining and they thought it "would pass quickly," but it did not. They never thought the river, which they were going to cross back home, was getting fuller all the time. It continued raining, and there was thunder and lightning. The night came and it became so dark. People were

Florence N. Mdlolo. *Political Violence, "Umlazi Grave Yard 1996,"* 2001–02. Cloth with embroidery and beadwork, 10.5" x 13.75", irreg.

stepping over stones, in the mud and others were slipping and falling all over the place. Others were holding on to the grass. Lightning was lighting the way. Children continued crying. Adults called their names and they responded.... But the adults could not get to the children because of the flooding. Help did not come because it's in the rural areas. Children drowned and the trees they were holding onto went down the river with them.

Embedded within each narrative is the hopelessness of being neglected by a social system, of having no safety nets, no infrastructure—not even the most minimal, such as sanitation facilities, telephones, and motor vehicles. What one learns from the project is the same as that derived from the recorded testimonies made to the Truth and Reconciliation Commission: All people who lived under apartheid "are wounded people."[8] Such tragedies resulted from having neither economic resources nor an understanding of how the white social system operates, nor access to those who did. It is ironic and devastatingly tragic that Florence N. Mdlolo died as a result of the same absence of infrastructure she writes about so lucidly.

The strength of the memory cloth project is that it captures complexity under the guise of simplicity, creating a safe environment in which women can tell these stories. It makes the equation between creativity, the reclamation of the past, and the development of consciousness while providing a form within which to give shape to the narration of tragedy—one important function of art.

Notes

An earlier version of this chapter appeared in *Art Journal* (Winter 2004).

1.   Florence N. Mdlolo suffered from asthma. On the day of her death, her asthma pump was depleted; they had been saving to buy a refill. They could not find anyone in her township to take her to the hospital. The one person with a vehicle wanted 500 rand to do so (the equivalent at the time of $50), and no one had the money to pay him. She finally was taken to the hospital after four hours had passed, but she was dead by the time they arrived.

2.   *After the TRC: Reflections on Truth and Reconciliation in South Africa,* ed. Wilmot James and Linda van de Vijver (Cape Town: David Philip Publishers, 2000), 4.

3.   Ibid., 63.

4.   *Amazwi Abesifazane* was started in 1999 by artist Andries Botha. It is still going strong under the auspices of Create Africa South. To date it has organized workshops in most of the South African provinces. Currently the workshops focus on the theme "A day I will never forget."

5.   *After the TRC,* 149.

6.   All personal accounts are taken from the *Amazwi Abesifazane* archive. Thanks to Andries Botha, Brenda Gouws, and Janine Zagel for making these available to me.

7.   *After the TRC,* 149.

8.   Ibid., 115

8
Gandhi's Body

✢

Location, Location, Location

Birla House

When invited to India to lecture in October 2003, I was thrilled. But the timing of the trip was such that I could only be gone from Chicago for ten days. In this short span, I had agreed to present three lectures in Mumbai (Bombay) and three in Delhi. Given my hectic schedule there was almost no time for sightseeing, but on my last day in Delhi and my *only* free afternoon, while rushing from place to place, I asked that we visit Birla House, the site where Gandhi was shot.

This location, memorializing the final event of Gandhi's life, set me on a path of passionate research. The results of my efforts, presented in this chapter, were inspired by that 2003 visit to a *location* that has become sanctified by several factors: Gandhi's residence during his final days, the assassination event itself, and the thousands who make secular and religious pilgrimages to Birla House, as I was doing, every year.

Let's begin at the end. By the time of his death, Gandhi's fasts, political negotiations, and actions of militant nonviolence had helped to transform British rule and determine the conditions for India's independence. The immediate events leading up to his assassination had perhaps been the most difficult in Gandhi's life. Of this period he said, "Time was when what I said went home.... Today mine is a cry in the wilderness."[1] Like others destined for prophecy, he felt, "When one's efforts do not bring forth results, one must dry up like a tree which does not bear fruit."[2] At this time Gandhi was horrified by the rage and violence accompanying the antagonisms between India and Pakistan, which arose for many reasons, among them the money owed Pakistan by India as a result of separation agreements, Prime Minister Jawaharlal Nehru's unwillingness to let go of Kashmir, and, of course, the religious intolerance between Muslims and Hindus. Thousands were dying as a consequence of this conflict.

Because Gandhi always had spoken well of Muslims and had insisted that Nehru and Home Minister Sardar Patel mediate, and not exacerbate, the struggles, his life became endangered not because of Muslim extremists but, rather, because of Hindu extremists who, instead of calling him "Mahatma," the great one or the great soul (a term Gandhi always rejected), had taken to calling him "Mohammed Gandhi" in mockery of his call for tolerance toward Muslims. To Hindu extremists he was a traitor responsible for the partition of India, the humiliation of his caste, and even the emasculation of his gender into "passive" resisters. As long as Gandhi was still alive, some felt India would never become the "modern" aggressive, forward-looking, and powerful state that certain factions desired. For these elements he stood in the way of "progress," defined as a new India taking leadership on an international scale, not with "militant nonviolence," a restraint that Gandhi had proposed and which he believed took the greatest courage, but with military strength.

When he arrived in Delhi on September 9, 1947, neither Nehru nor Patel believed it was safe for Gandhi to return to his former ashram. G. D. Birla, a wealthy industrialist who had been a devoted financial supporter of Gandhi's efforts, offered his home as a haven. He explained that Birla House had a large garden and an enclosed rear porch where several hundred could easily gather to hear Gandhi's prayers each day. Gandhi finally accepted these "elegant" accommodations because the Harijan Temple, his former home, was needed for the Punjabi refugees.

In an attempt to bring India back to sanity, Gandhi had gone on a long fast, in order, as he said, "to punish his [Gandhi's] impotent self for the general breakdown of Delhi, for the selfish corruption of the Congress, and for the criminal attacks against minorities in both dominions."[3] Because Gandhi's health was in danger, leaders from each community and party came together to promise to love and trust one another. He asked them to put their commitment to peace in writing. Thus the factions took a pledge to work together and to live like brothers in perfect amity.

But this truce did not last; underneath there was deep turmoil. On September 16, 1947, Hindu extremists had chanted "Death to Gandhi" when he insisted on using passages from the Koran in his prayers. And on January 20, 1948, he was so weak that he had to be carried out to offer his daily public ritual. During this meeting a bomb was detonated near the gathering, intended to be a diversion while an extremist rushed up to Gandhi and threw a grenade. But the terrorists lost heart. One was caught, while the others fled, plotting their return ten days later.[4]

Whenever Gandhi traveled throughout India, tens of thousands would stand on the road to get a glimpse of him. People wanted to "take his *darsan,*" a well-known tradition in which the holy person gives himself over to be *seen* by the villagers and the people "receive" their *darsan,* or a glimpse of the divine, through the evolved being in their midst.[5] On the day Gandhi was shot, January 30, 1948, Nathuran Godse, an upper-class, self-proclaimed devout Hindu, pushed through the crowd to be near Gandhi. Gandhi's young grandnieces attending him thought the man was rushing forward to be seen by Gandhi or even to touch him. Instead, Godse discharged three bullets from his pistol into Gandhi's naked chest. At first Gandhi kept moving forward supported by these two young women, whom he often referred to as his "walking sticks," until he crumpled to the ground at exactly 5:17 P.M., according to his watch, which had been smashed and stopped by his fall.

At Birla House there is now a small museum dedicated to a chronology of Gandhi's life, work, and death in several rooms of photos and timelines. There is also a display of the few objects Gandhi chose to possess in the end: the watch he was wearing on that fateful day, its glass face broken, frozen at the hour of his death; a room that re-creates his living quarters at the ashram—a plank bed, a spinning wheel, a pair of sandals; and the last photo of Gandhi's face, taken right after his death.

In the garden behind the museum, where, during his stay at Birla House, Gandhi held his public prayer meetings each afternoon at 5:00 P.M., there is a very simple memorial commemorating his last walk into the hands of his assassin. A series of raised footprints follows the path of his daily walk to prayers, like a river made of clay upon which his feet appear to float. These weighted clay steps mark the location where he touched the ground for the last time. The memorial thus alludes to the importance of *feet* in the Hindu tradition, in which they represent the incarnation of truly evolved beings who have entered into physical form. Great yogis and bodhisattvas like Buddha and Christ, it is believed, move *on* the earth but are not *of* the earth; are *in* the world but not *of* the world; are *with* us but not *of* us. Feet represent their worldly unworldliness, the location of the embodied spirit as it makes its mark on the earth. Feet were the first images used to represent the Buddha and the path to enlightenment. People rush to touch the feet of a prophet or a holy man, and some even drink the water used to bathe such feet, in the hope of receiving the guru's *shakti,* or energy.

The raised footprints in the garden behind Birla House also reflect Gandhi's determination, like that of Martin Luther King, Jr., decades later, to follow his chosen path, even knowing that it probably was leading him

Gandhi's Footprint Memorial at Birla House, New Delhi. *Photograph by Jessica Almy-Pagan.*

to destruction. At the time of his assassination, Gandhi was aware that his death was approaching. He used to say he wanted to live to be 125 years old, but when the Muslim-Hindu violence increased and would not be stopped, he no longer wanted to go on. At the end of his life he stood very much alone; he had rejected all offers of protection. And he did not fear death. "Rama," he said, "is my only protector ... if he wants to end my life, nobody can save me even if a million men were posted to guard me."[6]

Gandhi was a leader who spent his life perfecting discipline. For him, this was the key to all civilization. He rigorously cleansed his body and mind daily to prepare himself and others for an engaged life dedicated to what he understood as the search for truth that for him was always grounded in the specific fight against colonialism and the abuse of human rights. This saintly activist body that functioned as a witness of history and personal spiritual development was well honed to serve as an instrument of struggle and performative action as well as a site of reconciliation for hostile groups. It is therefore not surprising that of the multifarious aspects of Gandhi's life and character from which one can learn important lessons about the intersection of personal and political evolution, it is Gandhi's physical body transformed into image, symbol, and therefore location for the imagining of peace that I have been compelled to pursue.

The Scantily Clad Mahatma

In Erik Erikson's remarkable psychoanalytic profile of Gandhi, he quotes Gilbert Murray, who mused, "Gandhi would be a dangerous and uncomfortable enemy because his body, which you can always conquer, gives you so little purchase upon his soul."[7]

When we in the West think of Gandhi, we probably conjure the older Gandhi of historic photos, dressed simply in cotton, vigorous yet frighteningly thin, barelegged, and almost naked, meeting with dark-suited heads of state in cold, rainy climates like that of England. Or we imagine Ben Kingsley portraying him so perfectly that he has *become* Gandhi for several generations. It seems that as the actual Gandhi became more naked in appearance he also became more powerful in the world, yet we feel a bit embarrassed recalling him thus. Later in his life, when Gandhi wore only a loincloth and a shawl, there were those who observed that he folded his shawl over his body in a particularly careful way. He was in fact always meticulous about his appearance. So it is not surprising that in his early adult life, when a law student in London (1888–91), he so cultivated his "English Barrister" identity that he appeared in "silk hat and black coat .... and asked where he could get dancing lessons."[8] But it was only later, when Gandhi was in South Africa from 1893 to 1914 and employed as a lawyer presenting his first case, that his complex colonized appearance was contested.

Within the absurdities of South African racial categorizations, that Gandhi wore European clothing and also a turban at this time made his identity unclear and confusing to the presiding judge. The racist logic went like this: If he were an Indian Muslim, then he could pass as an "Arab," a fiction that Indians, Dutch, and British had agreed to maintain. An Arab, not being an "Asiatic," could have kept his turban on in the court, as did his companion. But only *Christian* Indians wore European clothes, and

Gandhi in Johannesburg, 1906. *Photograph copyright Vithalbhai Jhaveri/GandhiServe.*

they were usually waiters and clerks, not lawyers. Thus, a barrister wearing European clothing *and* a turban created a mixed racial and class message that made no sense in this context. Most Indians who had come to South Africa at this time had arrived as indentured laborers to work in the mines and fields for five years. These workers were called *coolies* or *samis,* and all Indians, no matter what their occupation, were lumped together by this term. Gandhi was therefore called a "coolie barrister."

As many people know, it was in South Africa where, while experiencing this cruelty of racial discrimination firsthand, his life's work became apparent to him. And it was there in the early 1890s that Gandhi, who had lived his entire life under British rule in India and in England and had been loyal to the British Empire, first became aware of the true nature of colonialism and that he was not a British subject with equal rights anywhere in the world. This epiphany took place on the often-recounted journey Gandhi made to Maritzburg in 1893.

Impeccably dressed in Western attire and on his way to a legal assignment in Pretoria, Gandhi was thrown out of the first-class compartment, for which he held a ticket, when the white man in his compartment refused to travel with him for the night. Ordered into third class, Gandhi refused, was thrown off the train, and then forced to sleep on a bench in the station on a very cold night without his overcoat. When Gandhi then tried to take a stagecoach to the *Transvaal,* the driver wanted to force him to sit at his feet on the floorboards. While attempting to book a hotel room, he was told that all hotels were filled. When a black American took him to his hotel, Gandhi was told he could have dinner there, but only if he ate in a room by himself. Embarrassed by the absurdity of the situation, the hotel owner finally arranged a place for Gandhi in the dining room with the other guests.

Gandhi's shock at the racial discrimination against Indians in South Africa manifested in these events was the impetus for his political and, ultimately, very personal spiritual awakening. As a result he even transformed his home into a hostel for those working for the cause of Indian rights and eventually redefined his family life as what appeared to be communal intimacy.

Later, when he returned home to India, clothing or the absence of it became even more politically significant. He began to spin cotton as part of the Indian Independence Movement's attempt to rely only on Indian-made goods. Gandhi then wore only *Kadhi,* the traditional plain Indian cotton. He also began to dress in a loincloth, or *dhoti,* identifying him thus with spiritually evolved beings and also with those who owned nothing more than a piece of cloth, especially after the anti-British demonstrations in which all foreign-made clothes were burned. In his last years he was usually bare-chested. When the famous Guru Paramhansa Yogananda finally met

Gandhi, he observed that although Gandhi was quite thin, his leanness was not in any way unpleasant "since his skin was very smooth and unwrinkled."[9] At this point, late in his life, it was surely this skin and not his clothing that dominated people's impressions of his physical appearance. His body, put increasingly in service of the collective good, attained an androgynous effect over time. Called both Father India (*Bapu*) and Mother India simultaneously, this androgyny became a source of embarrassment for certain groups of militant Hindu men.

Sexuality and Nonviolence

While we hold in our minds a postsexual or sexually neutralized image of Gandhi, in fact a great deal has been written about Gandhi's self-proclaimed youthful lustfulness and his decision at the age of thirty-seven, while living communally in South Africa, to become celibate, to attain *brachmacharya*, a necessary condition for self-realization within the ascetic Hindu tradition. This was a difficult decision for him and for his wife, Kasturba, who apparently was not initially consulted. He and Kasturba were wed in an arranged marriage when they were thirteen. Gandhi felt that by removing sexuality from his marriage, it would more likely be possible to treat his wife equally as a "helpmate, a comrade, and a partner."[10] This decision, although a personal one for Gandhi, was discussed in the public arena and presented as a challenge posed by himself to himself, one on which he could then be judged publicly as well.

Later in life, Gandhi, who was always in doubt about whether he had achieved true mastery over his passions, "tested" his ability to control his own desires by attempting to sleep next to naked young women without feeling any sexual urges. Manu, his cousin's nineteen-year-old granddaughter, was one of the young women who became part of these "experiments." In this and other ways she was very close to Gandhi and was with him when he was shot.[11] The result reassured Gandhi that he *could* control his lust. "His success in this respect (his advanced age could have been a factor) may have given him the moral strength to act with supreme courage ... in the face of the terrible division and carnage of those years [1946–47]."[12]

As problematic as such behavior now may seem, it fits within Gandhi's worldview and within the openness and rigor around issues of the body that existed in his ashrams. It was understood by all who lived near him that, for Gandhi, control of his body was a crucial reflection of his state of internal clarity, purity, and steadfastness. Because he believed violence to be a "function of the body," mastery of his body gave him the strength to fight against his own internal violence and thus, he believed, that of others.

The Hunger Artist

> You wish to know what the marks of a man are who wants to realize Truth
> which is God. He must reduce himself to zero and have perfect control
> over all his senses—beginning with the palate or tongue.
>
> Gandhi[13]

Among Gandhi's physical disciplines and personal renunciations, fasting
probably was the most directly relevant to the course of history. Each time
Gandhi made use of this strategy, there was high drama, especially toward
the end of his life, when, due to frail health, each fast had the potential to
become a fast to the death. There was always great power in these gestures
because, as Gandhi wrote, "Fasting is never intended to affect another's
body. It must affect his heart."[14] Since in the beginning at least there was
no question about the purity of Gandhi's motivations or his willingness to
give up his body, if necessary, for his beliefs, the fast became an incredibly
powerful strategy. Erikson writes, "The fast, begun on March 13, 1918, was
the first of seventeen fasts to the death, which Gandhi was to undertake
throughout his long life. In later years, all of India would hold its breath
while the Mahatma fasted, and whole cities would leave their lamps unlit
in the evening in order to be near him in the dark."[15]

This first fast was the result of his involvement in a mill worker's strike in
Ammadabad. The workers were asking for a 35 percent increase in wages.
At the point the workers were becoming dejected, Gandhi proclaimed, "I
cannot tolerate for a minute that you break your pledge. I shall not take any
food, nor use a car till you get 35 per cent increase or all of you die fighting
for it."[16] Feeling despondent before, the workers were galvanized by Gandhi's
pronouncement. This was Gandhi's aim: to stir the strikers' resolve through
his actions and help them recognize their potential power. Using the fast
to affect societal conflicts was a new concept for India. Its powerful effects
helped secure Gandhi's enormous spiritual presence in his own country and
the perception that he *embodied* great consciousness and the highest ideals
of the national and international character.

Throughout his life Gandhi also continued to fight for the just treatment of "untouchables"—those designated as low-caste Indians by upper-
class Hindus and thus discriminated against in extreme ways. Because
Gandhi abhorred anything that continued to separate untouchables from
other Hindus, he undertook another fast in 1932, this time while he was
in prison, having been arrested six days after his return from the second
set of roundtable discussions in England. Angry with the British, who had
agreed to hold elections for a bloc of separate seats on the new electorate
to candidates born only in "untouchable" communities, he once again
swore to fast to the death. Many were concerned about his health and

the monitoring of the fast in prison. To them Gandhi replied, "If the Hindu mass mind is not yet prepared to banish *untouchability* root and branch, it must sacrifice me without the slightest hesitation."[17] Hindu leaders convened conferences on the issue, and on September 25, 1932, they presented a statement: "No Hindu should be regarded as untouchable by reason of his birth."[18] On September 26, when Gandhi broke his fast, his weight had fallen to ninety-three pounds. Many Hindus and politicians denounced Gandhi's obsession with the issue of untouchability, since they saw it as a question of Hindu orthodoxy. But Gandhi refused to make these distinctions; he understood *all* infringements on civil liberties to be both spiritual and political.

For a time, Gandhi's long fasts in protest of the hatred and fighting between Hindus and Muslims *did* cause the violence to cease. This was true of his fast in Calcutta (1947) in the wake of postpartition communal violence. The fast only lasted five days, since communal leaders pledged themselves to prevent violence from erupting again in their city. But there did come a time toward the end of his life when these gestures of bodily renunciation no longer succeeded in the political arena. He had lost the power to temper violence with his own determination, peace, and meditation.

But Gandhi's fasts also had a spiritual purpose—referencing the concept of emptiness, and of emptying the self, an imperative at the heart of "all the great traditional forms of contemplative wisdom."[19] Gandhi believed that, as humans, we "should eat only as much as we need and no more.... Nature abhors a vacuum is only partially true." He commented, "Nature constantly demands a vacuum. The vast space surrounding us is the standing testimony of the truth."[20] He continued, "We should not put any partition between ourselves and the sky—the infinite.... If our bodies could be in contact with the sky without the intervention of houses, roofs, and even clothes, we are likely to enjoy the maximum amount of health.... This train of thought taken to the extreme, leads us to a condition where even the body becomes an obstacle separating man from the infinite."[21]

This concept of *Akash*, which might be taken as the "empty space surrounding the earth and the atmosphere around it,"[22] fascinated Gandhi. The chosen emptiness of the stomach, the emptying and abnegation of the ego, the nakedness and reduction of the flesh were deliberate acts of renunciation that created space within which Gandhi could reject the seductions of the world to commune with another. "If I succeed in emptying myself utterly," Gandhi wrote, "God will possess me."[23]

Salt

Whether Gandhi was truly a great spiritual and moral leader or a manipulative, cunning, strategic activist, all of these, or none, he rightly saw in the

Gandhi walking with journalists in Rome, December 13, 1931. *Photograph copyright Vithalbhai Jhaveri/GandhiServe.*

outrageous tax on salt an issue whose exposure would clearly unveil the absurdity of British rule in India. People needed salt to make their food palatable and also to sustain their bodies in India's heat. The salt tax affected the poorest of Indians and was particularly galling since salt was both omnipresent and easily collectible. It came to Gandhi in a dream that salt was to be the next action. And it was from this historic march and others that Gandhi earned his reputation as someone with great physical stamina, an energetic walker, leaving journalists and others much younger trailing behind him.

On March 12, 1930, Gandhi's followers—the *Satyagrahi*—planned to walk twelve miles a day for twenty-four days from the ashram at Sabarmati to the sea, while accumulating many supporters along the way. Once at the sea they would defy the British tax law by simply picking up salt from the salt flats. At the same time thousands up and down the coast of India would do the same.

On April 6, 1930 when Gandhi and 2,000 others reached the sea ... [Gandhi] ... dipped his bare legs in the water and then picked up a lump of salt that had dried on the sand. Voices yelled *Jai* or Victory. Several marchers were arrested on April 7 at the Village of Aat, four miles from Dandi. Police tried to remove the salt from the fingers of those civil resisters and one man's wrist was broken. The entire village then rushed to the scene, and women and children all began to dig for salt.[24]

Next, there was a full-scale plan to raid the salt beds at Dharasana. Finally, Gandhi was taken at night by train one hundred miles to prison. When this was known, large-scale protests began. By year's end 60,000 *Satyagrahis* had been arrested (Nehru was one of the first). After this police massacre against the protesters at the salt reserves at Dharasana, it became clear that British rule in India would have to end. "The Salt Satyagraha had demonstrated to the world the nearly flawless use of a *new instrument* of peaceful militancy."[25]

Satyagraha, an invented term, has been translated to mean both truth and force, and truth as force. However it is interpreted, "Satyagraha always includes the body and the meeting of bodies: the facing of the opponent 'eye to eye,' the linking of arms in defensive and advancing phalanxes, the body on the line. All these confrontations symbolize the conviction that the solidarity of unarmed bodies remains a leverage and a measure even against the cold and mechanized gadgetry of the modern state."[26] Gandhi writes, "Satyagraha postulates the conquest of the adversary by suffering in one's own person."[27]

"If I do not obey the law, and accept the penalty for the breach, I use soul-force. It involves sacrifice of the self," writes Gandhi.[28] He put his faith in the ability of his own body and soul and the collective body and soul to withstand the consequence of militant nonviolence and to elicit compassion in others when they observe those protestors willing to suffer without retaliation. "Real suffering bravely born," he believed, "melts even a heart of stone."[29] And it must be remembered that it was finally Gandhi's murder, the ultimate sacrifice of the body that "more than any other single event, finally brought an end to India's civil war."[30]

Turning the Inside Out

"As to the Mahatma's private life all we can say," writes Erikson, "is that here was a man who both lived and wondered aloud."[31] As modern as the character of Gandhi might appear in many of his attitudes about race, class, and, even later in his life, about gender, and as transparent as he insisted on being in relationship to issues of the body and his personal hygiene, as well as the degree to which he saw his life as a series of verifiable "experiments in truth," there are many who would say he was not a figure of modernity at all, in the Western sense, in part because for Gandhi there was no private self. Gandhi's weaknesses and transgressions were for him struggles with morality. These he shared with the public, but his interiority, which was not so much for him a monologue as a dialogue with God, he insisted on keeping to himself. Dipesh Chakrabarty writes, "The Gandhian private is nonnarratable and nonrepresentable. Not that it does not exist, but it is beyond representation."[32]

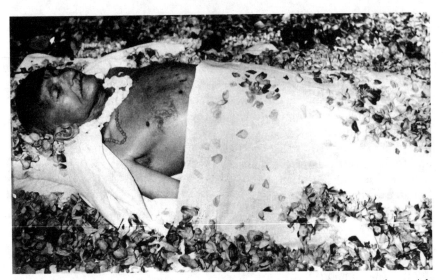

Gandhi on his deathbed, covered with flowers, January 31, 1948. *Photograph copyright Vithalbhai Jhaveri/GandhiServe.*

In this sense, he did not turn his inner self out into what in the Christian or even modernist sense might have been understood as confession. So, in all but this, he did try to fuse the private and the public, and to focus all his attention on the pursuit of truth and the liberation of India from British rule. He did not attempt to bring his personal life into the public, but rather to bring the public into his private existence. But he knew he must nonetheless always protect the inner voice that directed him, which he believed could best be heard in silence.

In Hannah Arendt's construct, Gandhi might be understood as a "selfless actor" whose actions were always a response to the world.[33] In Erich Fromm's sense, he was truly of "revolutionary character,"[34] committed always to humanity that went far beyond any parochial fixation with his own culture. Gandhi's entire development was based on action in the world, and each action was determined by witnessing injustice, whether it be the discrimination against Indians and all people of color in South Africa, or of the untouchables in India that he called *Harijans* (God's children), or the exploitation of peasants and workers by upper-class Indians, and finally the abuse of all these groups by the British during colonial rule. Such struggles to transform anger and hatred into compassion were acted out daily and deliberately through his body.

When he could no longer intuit how to stop the violence between Muslims and Hindus, or how to give the leadership of Nehru and Patel greater courage and vision, Gandhi then saw his life's work as a failure. And for him to fail in the public arena was to lose purpose. Because his identification with his own body and the body politic was complete, this sense of failure weakened his physical and spiritual bodies as well as his will. Yet his approach to conflict spread and lived beyond the *Satyagraha* movement through what anthropologists might refer to as "diffusion." "Gandhian" thus became an adjective, later attached to and adopted by significant leaders such as Martin Luther King, Jr.; Petra Kelly, head of the progressive Green party in Germany (both of whom died violently); and César Chávez, one of the founders of the United Farm Workers Union.

These struggles shared the core concept that those without power can acquire power if they are able to control their actions and operate principally within the boundaries of nonviolent noncooperation—putting one's total humanity, vulnerability, and, particularly, one's body at the mercy of others in the hope that these fellow humans might be moved to consciousness by such determination of action and selfless physical sacrifice. This is not a practice for everyone but for those who, like Gandhi, were able to, as he says, "arrive at the ideal of total renunciation and learn to use the body for the purpose of service."[35]

It is arguable that Gandhi presents in his image both an "imperishable" representation of truth, tradition, the stability of the world and our experience of it,[36] as well as a representation of the one who acts spontaneously and whose gesture of personal perfection is linked to new paradigms of unprecedented social transformation. Using Thomas Merton's articulation, we might say that Gandhi does not *react* but rather *responds,* involving his whole being in his action and taking full responsibility for its effect.[37] He is like an artist who functions philosophically and creates in his person a symbolic universe in direct relationship to the historical context.

In this way Gandhi's actions, in their clarity and reliance on performative gesture—the fast, the march, the dress, the look, and the complete and deliberate control of and engagement with the body when conceptualized as response to existing societal conditions—mirror the act and effect of deliberate art making, creating a *location* within which the symbolic is constructed and ideas can be contemplated.

The Controlled Illusion That Heals[38]

The House with the Ocean View

In November 2002 artist Marina Abramovic, known for her extreme actions dependent on risk and the transformation of her private body into a public body, her internal space of contemplation into an external one, *responded,* once again. This time she did so in a piece titled *The House with the Ocean View.* Stripping her world to the barest essentials, she gave herself the task of living in New York's Sean Kelly Gallery for twelve days, with very circumscribed action. To quote Thomas McEvilley's comprehensive essay on this performance:

> [Abramovic] was on the set for 271 consecutive hours and on display to the public for 118. The passage of time was ticked off, at about one beat a second, by a metronome.... This was the action: Abramovic would walk, stand, sit and lie down, draw a glass of water from the faucet installed over her bed and drink it, standing in a particular place and angled in a particular way to the light; urinate and wipe herself with toilet paper; take the hair band from the shelf, walk into the bathroom, put on her hair band, remove her clothes, take a shower, get out of the shower, dry her body with a large towel, put her clothes back on, remove the headband, walk back to the bedroom and replace the hair band on the hidden shelf. If you stayed for two or three hours you'd probably see all this.[39]

McEvilley understands her actions as a reflection of the principle presented by French artist Yves Klein, who said, "The artist only has to produce one work, himself [herself], constantly."[40]

Abramovic creates emptiness, or *"Akash,"* as an exercise in purification of the body and the mind. Like Gandhi, Abramovic, in this performance, seemed obsessed with cleanliness, taking three showers a day during the twelve days designated for fasting, cleansing, and clearing out the body as well as the spirit. After twelve days the gallerists put a functional ladder against the set, and Abramovic calmly, undramatically climbed down to drink a glass of orange juice—thus ending the performance. No fuss, no fanfare, no crowds.

The core of the piece was in its simplicity and elegance, as well as the unconditional commitment that Abramovic brings to all her work. Its austerity was symbolic. The knives whose blades faced up served as the rungs of the ladders that forbade her from coming down from her perch. One recalls Kafka's "Hunger Artist," who was theatrically locked inside his cage with a big padlock by the impresario, so the audience would believe that he could not sneak food.[41] Those sharp blades made it clear that Abramovic could not and would not walk down from her perch before the designated time. But neither the "Hunger Artist" nor Abramovic would *dare* sneak food. Like Gandhi, their fasts have been designed to test and strengthen their own resolve. The audience is only the occasion for and the witness to the control of their bodies, spirits, and wills.

Abramovic's set was here composed of three stages that appeared as an altar and also created the affect and effect of a "triptych of domestic essentials," as RoseLee Goldberg has written.[42] We were given a painterly, frontal view and, as in such tripartite paintings, every visual detail was considered in relationship to the whole. The palette was manifest in Abramovic's change

Marina Abramovic. *The House with the Ocean View.* 2002, Sean
Kelly Gallery, New York. *Artwork copyright Marina Abramovic;
photograph provided by Sean Kelly Gallery, New York.*

of costume—red, blue, white, and gold against the white walls, an allusion
to America perhaps, so desperately in need of healing in November 2002,
when the piece was performed in New York, only a year after the events of
September 11, 2001.

The House with the Ocean View was a utopian contrivance of course, but,
nevertheless, a performance designed to dissolve the plasma between self
and other, artist and audience, so we might encounter one another in our
physical and psychological nakedness as one species, unencumbered, in need
of quiet, deep contemplation, and the further evolution that could follow.

Here the visual artist created space by clearing space, so the mind of the
viewer might find peace and calmness while staring into her gaze, and allowing that gaze to dissolve the distance between truth and fiction, life and
art. Although there was no "performing" per se, there were exchanges of
energy. Abramovic said that it was when people came into the gallery that
she became most energized. Otherwise she was completely in her own mind
and in the space of the installation—a mirror of her own consciousness.

Stripped of most artifice, Abramovic's animalness and physical vulnerability were also on display. But McEvilley points out that she could be naked,
taking a shower, and still not elicit any lascivious reactions in her audience.
The dignified seriousness of her intention was apparent throughout. So
nakedness here was not the seduction of nudity, as in Berger's famous dis-
tinction,[43] but the body without artifice, *naked*. In *The House with the Ocean*

View the art making appears to be the art of making the self. "The desert reduces you to yourself," Abramovic wrote in her book *Public Body*. "That's all that happens."[44]

What results when an artist functions as a renunciate? Does she then also become a healer? Here Abramovic moved between the psychic and the physical, artifice and nature, "providing opportunities" for what Sudhir Kakar calls "the controlled illusion that heals."[45]

Witnessing Chaos

The psychic distance between the stripped-down contemplative world of Marina Abramovic's triptych performance to Susanna Coffey's exuberant paintings of war and devastation in Iraq and Haiti is not as great as may at first appear. Artists of depth, they each choose to witness and potentially affect the chaos of the world through their own person. Abramovic, utilizing her contemplative body, attempts to create an antithesis—the meditation temple in the Gallery. Coffey positions her constructed self-portraits in representational relationship to disaster—the persona as witness located within the vibrations of painting.

A portrait painter who has consistently presented a ravaged reinterpretation of her face as a landscape or topography, Coffey positioned this visage against the backdrop of journalistic war photos transformed and interpreted

Susanna Coffey. *Fall.* 2003, oil on panel, 27 x 36 in. *Artwork copyright Susanna Coffey. Photograph by David Allison.*

Susanna Coffey. *Night Vision #2.* 2003, oil on panel, 60 x 72 in.
Artwork copyright Susanna Coffey. Photograph by David Allison.

through paint to capture devastation with such exquisite totality that they
are reminiscent of Turner's *Burning of the House of Lords and Commons, October
16, 1834* or *Slavers Throwing Overboard the Dead and Dying—Typhoon Coming
Up, 1840.* But in these the painter puts a version of *herself* into these bombed-
out landscapes of fire and catastrophe, creating as she says, a "culpability
of presence."[46] She has created the nonportrait self-portrait, the body/self
as witness to humanity's atavistic fascination with violence and devastation.
These paintings capture the hidden forces of *Thanatos* (death instinct) and
the dark gods of war that live in the primal recesses of human consciousness, unable to evolve.

Like Abramovic's work, these paintings too may have been motivated by
the New York horrors of September 11, which took place close to Coffey's
home and studio in lower Manhattan. Could anyone who lived through
and absorbed the shock of that moment and its images, as she did, not have
internalized catastrophe on a grand and physical scale? But here Coffey's
intention is not to re-present *that* physical site, although she might disclose
or reopen it to our consciousness, but rather to represent Baghdad burning,
Haiti burning—two contemporary human-made disasters that she, and we,
were all witnessing at the time of this production.

The paintings allow us to observe the end of gravity and surely the end
of grace, as in *Fall,* where the sky appears to be tumbling to pieces onto an
already destroyed cityscape burnt to a crisp. These works create a perfect

"now"—no past, no future, just the present incendiary landscape, the moment of witnessing extended to eternity, dusting everything with the fine white, blue, or orange powder of dissolution. "Yet, chaos itself can be a germ of order," writes Daniel W. Smith in his introduction to Gilles Deleuze's study of Francis Bacon.[47] Order might emerge from this image of devastation, but only that of the deliberately structured painting itself and our reflection of its content.

Is this face peering out to us Everyman or Everywoman breathing in the heat of obliteration? Or is she the only human left to record what has occurred, like a *shade* in *The Inferno* gesticulating through the flames? Perhaps this is the last anchorwoman, telecasting to no one, dressed for the apocalypse in what appears to be a blue bathing cap or bandanna to match the surreal blue light? The afterglow of a planet destroyed? Camouflaged into the landscape, she has become the color of the painting. *We* are in the painting because *she* is in the painting. She appears alone as if there were no remaining human context. We provide the connection to other humans. Were there no figure, they would stand outside us, and we would not be implicated. How then would *we* witness the devastation up close? How would we put ourselves into the landscape? If this is hell we are visiting, it is the hell of war, a particularly human-made psychic and physical location.

As Klee advised, "Not to render the visible but to render visible."[48] The War Paintings, as I call these, like *The House with the Ocean View*, make visible a response of the entire being, crafted out of the freedom artists have to fabricate and then stand, outside, inside, or *on* the ground they have created, offering a topography within which the complexity of these catastrophic ideas about the self in an obliterated world can exist.

Strange Bedfellows

Gandhi, Abramovic, Coffey—strange bedfellows. Yet I have brought them together in order to discuss the power of the *person* to embody truth about war, violence, and peace, and the power of art to do the same.

Even in the case of Marina Abramovic, whose performances come through the body directly, it is the *persona* of the performer, not the *actual* person, whom we finally encounter in the public sphere. Such is the same with Susanna Coffey. However close the face in her paintings may or may not be to her actual self, one would not want to confuse these representations with her person. The images are solutions to the problem of representation. They are a way to approach or reveal something the artist wishes to communicate through a fabrication; they are not the thing itself.

On the other hand, Gandhi was a man in the world, not a work of art. In his case it is his life, person, persona, image, the representation of the image, his private body transformed into a public body—all of it—that is the object of scrutiny. It is the embodiment of ideas, a totality filled with contradictions but also made known and visible to us as an evolving *project*. Living his life's lessons as what he called "experiments in truth," reiterating over and again in gesture, "My life is my message,"[49] he attempted to perfect the self—not as an end in itself or an end in himself but as a means to an end. And one might say of Gandhi's body—as Picasso said of *Guernica*—that it too was an "instrument of war" whose goal was always "nothing less than world peace." The liberation of India was only the beginning of his struggle.[50] And to this day the peace movement in India and Pakistan conjures the name of Gandhi and returns to his teachings to bolster its struggle against those who would incite nationalism and nuclear aggression and equate masculinity with such unholy power.

The journey to understand why Gandhi's life ended in the garden of Birla House prompts me to ask, how can one learn from Gandhi's pursuit, from what he considered the "truth" of each situation? And how can one define such a pursuit in a post-postmodern age that even argues the possibility of truth? Gandhi asked himself such historically bound questions continuously, and at least one eternal one that the Greeks also recognized as essential to philosophical thought: How should one live?

Can we imagine, as Gandhi tried to do, one person at peace and then, by extension, can we conceive of a community at peace, a nation at peace, a world at peace? When did the desire for such attempted imaginings drop out of our collective hope for the future, or our intellectual, theoretical investigations, only to be *re-placed* by an acceptance, however unconscious, of endless or inevitable war—a cancer without a cure that can only be managed?[51]

As representations of the human desire for peace, the focus on such images as Gandhi's body and the work of Abramovic and Coffey may seem neoutopian and even naive. And yet they provide locations wherein an iconography essential for a resistant collective consciousness focused on the conditions for a just and humane society can be imagined.

Notes

This chapter is dedicated to the memory of my friend and colleague George Roeder—historian of war, advocate for peace. An earlier version of this chapter was published in *Art Journal* (Winter 2007).

1. Speech by Gandhi at prayer meeting, January 7, 1948, as quoted in Stanley Wolpert, *Gandhi's Passion: The Life and Legacy of Mahatma Gandhi* (London: Oxford University Press, 2001), 253.

2. Ibid., 244.

3. Ibid., 253.

4. David Arnold, *Gandhi: Profiles in Power* (London: Pearson Education Limited, 2001), 225.

5. Diana L. Eck, *Darsan: Seeing the Divine Image in India,* 3rd edition (New York: Columbia University Press, 1998), 6.

6. Wolpert, *Gandhi's Passion,* 255.

7. Erik H. Erikson, *Gandhi's Truth: On the Origins of Militant Nonviolence* (New York, W.W. Norton, 1969), 391.

8. Ibid., 147.

9. Paramhansa Yogananda, *Autobiography of a Yogi,* "With Mahatma Gandhi at Wardha" (Los Angeles: Self-Realization Fellowship, 1946), 497–517.

10. Erikson, *Gandhi's Truth,* 235.

11. David Hardiman, *Gandhi in His Time and Ours: The Global Legacy of His Ideas* (New York: Columbia University Press, 2003), 105.

12. Ibid.

13. When in the midst of working on this issue of Gandhi's body, I discovered a book with what might appear to be a similar orientation, yet with ultimately a different intention. However, I have found its insights fascinating. I first saw this quote of Gandhi in Joseph S. Alter, *Gandhi's Body: Sex, Diet, and the Politics of Nationalism* (Philadelphia: University of Pennsylvania Press, 2000), 44.

14. Ibid., 43.

15. Erikson, *Gandhi's Truth,* 351.

16. Ibid.

17. Wolpert, *Gandhi's Passion,* 16.

18. Ibid., 168.

19. Thomas Merton, *Mystics and Zen Masters* (New York: Farrar, Straus and Giroux, 1961), 212.

20. Alter, *Gandhi's Body,* 41.

21. Ibid., 39.

22. Ibid.

23. Ibid., 48.

24. Wolpert, *Gandhi's Passion,* 148.

25. Erikson, *Gandhi's Truth,* 447.

26. Ibid., 198.

27. Louis Fischer, ed., *The Essential Gandhi: An Anthology of His Writings on His Life, Work, and Ideas* (New York: Vintage Spiritual Classics, 1962), 78.

28. Ibid.

29. Ibid., 79.

30. Dennis Dalton, *Mahatma Gandhi: Nonviolent Power in Action* (New York: Columbia University Press, 1993), xvii.

31. Erikson, *Gandhi's Truth,* 404.

32. Dipesh Chakrabarty, *Habitations of Modernity: Essays in the Wake of Subaltern Studies* (Chicago: University of Chicago Press, 2002), 62.

33. Hannah Arendt, *Responsibility and Judgment* (New York: Schocken, 2003). See the Introduction by Jerome Kohn, vii–xxix.

34. Erich Fromm, *The Dogma of Christ: And Other Essays on Religion, Psychology, and Culture* (New York: Henry Holt and Company, 1955). See the chapter "The Revolutionary Character," 147–66.

35. Fischer, *The Essential Gandhi,* 56.

36. Arendt, *Responsibility and Judgment,* xxvii.

37. From Merton, *Mystics and Zen Masters,* 250: "Here we must remember that *response* is something more than *reaction.* Response involves the whole being of man in his freedom and in his capacity to 'see' and 'move on.' Reaction is nothing more than the mechanical, perhaps astutely and dishonestly improvised, answer of one's superficial self."

38. Sudhir Kakar, *The Analyst and the Mystic: Psychoanalytic Reflections on Religion and Mysticism* (Chicago: University of Chicago Press, 1991), 25.

39. Thomas McEvilley, "Performing the Present Tense," *Art in America* 91, no. 4 (April 2003), 114–17.

40. Ibid.

41. Franz Kafka, "A Hunger Artist," in *The Penal Colony: Stories and Short Pieces* (New York: Schocken, 1961), 243–56.

42. RoseLee Goldberg, "The Theater of the Body," in *Marina Abramovic:* The House with the Ocean View (Milano: Charta, 2002), 157.

43. John Berger, *Ways of Seeing* (New York: BBC and Pelican, 1972), 57–64.

44. Marina Abramovic, *Public Body: Installation and Objects: 1965–2001* (Milano: Charta, 2001), 184.

45. Kakar, *The Analyst and the Mystic,* 25.

46. Emile Ferris, *F News,* School of the Art Institute of Chicago, "The Beauty of Tragic Times: Interview with Susanna Coffey," September 2004, 20–21.

47. Gilles Deleuze, *Francis Bacon: The Logic of Sensation,* introduction by Daniel W. Smith (Minneapolis: University of Minnesota Press, 2002), xx.

48. Cited in ibid., xxiii.

49. There are many tales about the origin of this quote. One is that when a journalist came up to Gandhi's train as it was pulling out of the station and asked Gandhi what his message to the world was, Gandhi wrote on a piece of paper and handed it through the window. On it was written, "My life is my message." In any case, this quote appears on at least two statues of Gandhi that I saw in South Africa, one in Pietermaritzburg and one in Durban.

50. Yogananda, *Autobiography of a Yogi,* 516.

51. I refer readers to Paul Virilio, in particular to the essay "Pure Power." This can be found in the Semiotext(e) edition of *Popular Defense and Ecological Struggles,* trans. Mark Polizzotti (New York: 1990), but also in the *Paul Virilio Reader,* ed. Steve Redhead (New York: Columbia University Press, 2004), 45–56.

9
Acqua Alta

⌇

This is an essay about emptiness. It begins in Venice, a dream surrounded by water from which one does not want to awaken.[1]

The Blank Wall

We checked into a hotel that had once been a convent—an old facade with an interior now overdesigned and seriously hip—on a side street near the Accademia bridge on a stormy day in June. They gave us the key, number twenty-seven, up two flights and around two corners. After struggling to line up the eye of my fish-shaped electronic key with the green dot on the wall, I entered the room and immediately approached the windows to see the view, a reflex of travelers entering hotel rooms around the world, anxious to fulfill the expectation that the time away from home—the two days, two weeks, two months of reprieve from regular daily life—will pass like a dream.

There were new beautiful, large wood-framed windows on the south wall that opened from the tops and from the sides. There were layers of drapes with gray on lighter gray mermaids blowing brocade bubbles, and there were electric metallic shades that came down when you pressed the switch (which I did inadvertently whenever I wanted to shut off the reading light). In truth there were so many lights that it took a week to figure out how to turn everything on and off. But when I cleared all this away, I looked out to discover that our extravagant room was facing a blank wall separated by a

High water in Piazza San Marco, St. Mark's Square, Venice, 2006.
Photograph by Carol Becker.

small winding street. The wall, however, was such a subtle milky white that at first I thought it was sky. When our windows were closed, it appeared that we were looking out on calm white water or a cloud. It was reminiscent of a James Turrell *Skyspace*—a cutout of the ceiling or wall at just the right angle so that it allows one to remove all distinct boundaries, see oneself seeing, and then notice and reflect upon the color of light.

But, even with all this, I still was not seduced. Desperate to see Venice, I ran downstairs and asked if we could change rooms. "No, signora, there are no other rooms, not until Tuesday. You must understand you have one of our best rooms." "But it has no view," I said. "It looks out on a wall." The young hotel clerk, dressed in a black velvet vest with sparkled insets, white shirt, black pants, and gray silk ascot—the elegant uniform of the hotel— looked at once bemused and horrified. "But signora," he said, "what a wall it is. That is the back wall of the Accademia. On the other side of that wall are the Carpaccios. If we drill a hole into the wall one night, we could steal many of the great paintings of Venice. That is a special wall." I went back upstairs, opened the window, looked down at the small street beside the hotel and then to the wall. When it opened at 8:15 the next morning, I was the first in line at the Accademia.

In the early 1800s this complex of buildings became a museum housing the most important collection of fourteenth- to eighteenth-century Venetian paintings. There was no one but me and the guards at that early hour, so I walked right through to the large interior space, visually overwhelmed by the plethora of martyrs, Virgins, images of the baby Jesus again and again, representations of sixteenth-century Venetian iconography, unable to stop until I got to *my* wall. And when I reached the back of the Accademia, what did I find? On my wall was not in fact Carpaccio's famous cycle of the "Legend of St. Ursula," as my hotel clerk had said. On my wall were the equally fabulous Tintorettos and Tiepolos.

Here reside the worst of gravity and the best of grace. Angels hung upside down in impossibly blue skies, their skirts miraculously never blown over their heads. St. Mark (*San Marco*) dropped from the heavens, hovering with great bravado over an all-too-human scene of exploitation, extending his hand to free a slave being tortured. San Marco again, this time in the act of *being* saved by two Venetian tradesmen using the opportunity of an unexpected storm to whisk his body to safety from the massive pyre prepared for its immolation. In this painting, people are in retreat, fleeing up the steps into the Doges' palace, grasping onto anything to keep them from being swept up by the wind. (During our time in Venice we would experience such a storm. When the rain began unexpectedly and lashed horizontally, drenched tourists and Venetians alike tried to escape the torrent by running into churches, jumping onto empty *vaporettos* [water taxis]. We were on a large boat going to Torcello when the storm hit, so we disembarked in Barano and ducked into a crowded café to drink hot chocolate, thick as syrup, until the rain subsided.)

In the same room, but on an adjacent wall, hung one of the largest paintings ever made, which hundreds of years before had been repatriated from France. This painting, once known as a version of the *Last Supper,* had been understood as heretical in its day. Paolo Veronese, refusing to make the changes to his painting that the church requested, simply changed its title to *Christ in the House of Levi*—a sixteenth-century painting filled with the iconography of its time, Christ in a Venetian villa outrageously feted by noblemen. (Whatever happened to fasting in the desert?)

However grandiose the scale and quality of these paintings, the narrative possibilities throughout the galleries are both limited and surreal. One is either already a saint, on the way to becoming a saint and therefore in danger of immolation, crucifixion, or all of the above, or in the process of being saved by saints who often hover, elevated (as they should be) above the physical plane. Here we have entered the dreams and nightmares of the sixteenth century, when artists were the recorders of "histories"—both real or imagined—that haunted the collective psyche, when artists were the assigned re-presenters of the contemporary landscape. Here, at the height of Venetian civilization, marvelously chronicled, is the uncivilized behavior of humans materialized through the grandeur of large-scale narrative paintings. These are paintings as large as any movie screen inside or out, saturated with images—fierce, complex, unimaginable, mythic, recognizable images for the audiences of the time; paintings that five centuries later still have the power to seep into our psyches and match our dreams, that still have the power to animate and give meaning to the blank milky white stucco walls that contain them inside and out.

Room 5 in the interior of the Accademia is devoted to the Bellini depictions of the Virgin and child. Here are the most magnificent clear-faced Virgins and world-weary babies Jesus ever painted. On one small wall are hung two paintings with disparate depictions of Christ at extreme stages of his time on earth. But it is the empty space between these paintings that haunts me. The Bellinis are not on the back of *my* wall but on yet another wall where the blankness again becomes a source of imagining. Overtaken by an odd obsession probably known to art historians around the world, one begins to memorize and take comfort in knowing exactly *where* such unearthly paintings actually reside in physical space—which city, museum, room, and even which wall.

So, on one side of a small interior space, on a truncated inner wall only two paintings are hung. One is a painting called *Madonna col Bambino—El Battista* (The Baptism). In this painting a beautiful young mother Mary, looking out from the canvas, holds her baby Jesus upright on her lap, proud of this perfect, voluptuous boy. Here is innocence, health, adoration—the beginnings of an allegory that has captured the imaginations of spiritual people across religions for centuries. Next to this painting is a small blank space and then another Bellini painting called *Pietà*. In this painting, a much older aggrieved Virgin sits in the foreground of a symbolic landscape that winds back to a church steeple. Across her lap she cradles her martyred son, now a full-sized bearded man, still naked except for a small white cloth across his pelvis. He is emaciated, his eyes rolled back in their sockets, his arms dangling limp on either side and scarred by stigmata, *her* face haggard, in pain, looking down at his body. All that marks the catastrophe that has taken place between these paintings is the decimated condition of these principal characters and a small respectful space on the wall. But in that space, representative of the unarticulated duration from adoration to martyrdom, everything has already happened—a drama the world still has not absorbed, an event Wilhelm Reich called the first massacre of the individual by the mass.[2]

This beautiful child has become a man. The man has claimed to be the Son of God. For such claims he has been crucified—the perfect body destroyed by the rage of men. Here Mary looks at her dead son as any mother might—what have they done to my boy? What *have* they done to my boy? From the adoration of the child to the destruction of the man, the dream becomes manifest, the dream becomes nightmare, the child becomes the man she could not save, the man becomes the fulcrum point for the spiritual life of millions, all in her gesture, in her look, and in the resignation of the dead body limp across her lap—the evidence of his life on earth. In the

Giovanni Bellini, *Pietà*, c. 1500, 65 x 87 cm.

narrative not offered, in the narrative unpainted, in the space left empty resides the magnitude of the all-too-human catastrophe.

Erasure

About Hiroshi Sugimoto's series "Theaters," photos of luminous white screens in vacant deco theaters and drive-ins, Adrian Heathfield writes, "The space which occupies the center of the frame is not an empty space waiting to be filled, but a space which has already been filled; a space of erasure. This is then a still whose stillness is in question; what the still image 'holds' is a particular duration, whose visibility is absent in the captured image. What is evidently obliterated here is animation and time's succession."[3] It is not simply *white* light that splashes on to the ceiling, to the proscenium floor, to the edges, to the banisters, and even to the space in front of the first row of chairs that illuminates Sugimoto's magnificently voided theater screens. It is, rather, a luminous and ghostly light that fills the space—an emptiness mirrored in the vacant chairs that allude to the absent audience and that is everywhere palpable. It is light mirrored in the aisles, which reminds us that humans move through this space up to the screen. And it is through these aisles that our eyes also move into the darkness of the photo to meet the light that appears as a sacred icon at the center of the temple. Heathfield continues, "What is evidently obliterated here is animation and time succession. This erasure of cinematic spectacle takes place in the very site where vision has been excessively practiced, as if it were that excess of looking that causes the erasure of the image."[4] Does Heathfield mean that looking too hard makes it impossible to see?

This is a full emptiness, a voided emptiness, a sense of something once there that is now gone. Forgetting through repression *is such erasure*. It is absence with presence. Traumatic information is never really gone; it may be obscured, hidden, dissolved, distorted, recoded, reabsorbed; it may affect everything we do; yet it often cannot be consciously recalled. Such blankness creates a gnawing sense that something once there is now gone, a thing once known is now unknown. Encountering what has been repressed and therefore forgotten thus becomes uncanny—something once known, then hidden, that now makes itself manifest once again. Something one experiences as familiar. But why? Such re-cognition embodies the unconscious memory of its own obfuscation.

Waiting for a *vaporetto* in Venice, I describe the Sugimoto photographs to a friend, media critic Daniel Dayan. I talk about the empty screens and their potential meaning, and I ask for his interpretation. Almost immediately he says two words: "erasure" and then "Oedipus." "Yes," I say, "that which must be taken away because its meaning is too great." "This is not simply white light," Heathfield quotes Sugimoto as saying, "it is the result of too much information."[5] Sugimoto sets the aperture wide open and leaves it that way for the duration of the film. In the end there is so much information that it erases itself. It is not really emptiness, but, rather, an overwrought fullness.

The *vaporetto* arrives, and the conversation dissolves in its wake.

Tragedy

Oedipus had spent his life fleeing from the oracle's declaration that he would kill his father and marry his mother. In leaving what he thought was his original home and his biological parents, he thought he could escape the curse. But of course the nature of Greek destiny is that you never can be free of that which you carry inside you. Still caught in your own humanity, you believe that you alone can outwit the fates. Such *hubris* or pride inevitably destroys everything and everyone who comes in contact with the cursed protagonist. When the blind prophet Tiresias alludes to the truth at the source of the plague destroying the people of Thebes—"You are the pollution," he says to the king—Oedipus begins to suffer this hidden knowledge.

In the Tyrone Guthrie film (1957) of the stage production, the chorus begins chanting "Oedipus, Oedipus." Voices from a distance call for his presence, as if his name, which alludes to the pierced ankles bound when he was an infant, could conjure his history. He senses what is known to him unconsciously—his body-knowledge, a truth understood in some part of the self that the conscious mind cannot yet bring to awareness. As Oedipus's intimate, from the Latin *intimus,* "in most," Tiresias intimates the truth. He hints at the cause of the plague. He intimates an inmost, intimate knowledge, fully aware that to announce it would be to overwhelm Oedipus with information that as yet he cannot allow himself to consciously know or completely absorb, lest it absorb him. When Oedipus finally recognizes that he has killed his father, Laertes, married his mother, Jocasta, and fathered four children with her, his response is to pierce his eyes, to guarantee that he will no longer see the results of all that he has already violated. He accomplishes this with the sharp ends of two brooches, which he rips from the body of Jocasta, his wife-mother, who already has hung herself, aware before he is of her defilements. And, as in all great Greek tragedies, this horrific act occurs off stage. We are only *told* that it has taken place. When we see Oedipus next, his eyes are oozing a thick, black liquid. Already blind, Oedipus seeks to obliterate all images, but, like King Lear who follows, without his eyes he sees the painful truth even more clearly.

If there has ever been a moment of information overload, this was it. The burden of remembering all that has occurred threatens to obliterate Oedipus with its gravity. No upside-down angels descend to save him. No grace, no redemption, no erasure; just the overwhelming weight of his sins against the gods. He can either die or become a prophet.

At the center of Greek tragedy is its role in the collective healing process. There was the assumption that these massive catastrophes (in Greek *katastrophes*—overturnings) would replicate the worst disasters imaginable to the unconscious, that they would electrify the hidden desires, taboos, repressions of the *polis* and would end with a *catharsis* (cleansing) that would benefit all. At a deep unconscious level, such a theatrical spectacle was the vehicle for psychological projection. Adhering to Aristotelian concepts of the nature and function of tragedy and of the hierarchy of authority in relationship to the masses, the king's worst nightmare—his violation of the taboos of both incest and patricide—frees the populace from their own longings to commit such crimes, and it was assumed that for a time these desires could be assuaged by the conscious re-cognition of their consequences and function as a useful safety valve for maintaining social cohesion.

Projection here is associated with deep psychological manifestations. Yet, like Sugimoto's luminous whiteness, it can contain an overdetermined meaning that ultimately whites itself out. In its other contexts, projection can refer to superficial two-dimensional or ghostlike images that can easily be ignored, covered up, assimilated, manipulated, or erased.

Obsession

In another work about erasure, British artist Tim Etchells, best known for his involvement with the company Forced Entertainment, has directed a movie titled *Starfucker*. In it he replaces all filmic images with the black-and-white void of after-hours television and text. Here is language that re-creates scenarios between famous movie stars so that we, the audience, must conjure the images ourselves to fill the vacuum Etchells has provided. Adrian Heathfield is correct to see the loss of the physical body replaced by the illusion of enactment, manifestation, and the tease of the absented visual as an extreme fascination with Hollywood and its stars. Heathfield writes, "What language evokes in *Starfucker* is a failed substitute, not the discrete body, but the body in various states of disarray and excess, the body losing itself within and against the proprieties of the cinematic."[6]

In a sense the genre to which Etchells refers, Hollywood films, could be defined as those films that represent the cult of the star as opposed to the actor/actress, elevate glamour to the status of content, portray projection as epiphany, substitute climax for the healing force of catharsis—all of which can satisfy at only one level and can rarely resonate at the depth of psychological projection and identification that would make these films personally or socially significant. There is therefore no corporeal or intellectual satisfaction. To remove the visual, as Etchells has done, is to leave it all to our own imaginations and allow us to project, visually, on to the names of these stars the personalities we associate with these names and to force us into our own banal form of identification. Etchells withholds the visual action from us, as these films withhold the depth of artistic intention. He creates virtual hits of vicariousness.

But it is not a world, as Heathfield notes, gone back to the importance of narrative and storytelling *before* we were overwhelmed by the visual in motion. Rather, it is a world returned to the language of narrative *after* visual narrative, and our own potential imaginings for it have been exhausted by Hollywood's poisonous banality—after the physical has been depleted. It is not a world like that of the tragedies that spares us the visual horror of psychic pain, the psychic pain of visual horror; rather, it is a world incapable of such depth of emotion. Etchells depicts a post-Hollywood world of sensual deprivation in which we are left with a visually blank black-and-white screen where once action, romance, visual illusion dominated. Now we are no longer seduced through the senses but only irritated by the endless unsatisfying possibilities constructed in language, leading only to the realization of the impoverishment of our own projections that twist like the ouroborous, forever back onto themselves.

This is not Sugimoto's overstimulated world of elegant luminosity, represented as mystery, icon, the unknown, the unoccupied, the once present now erased. Nor is this the blank wall of the Accademia, with all the enormous possibilities it generates for fantasizing its penetration through the dramatic world of epic narrative energized through paint, the dream of religion, and the mythic imaginings of sublimity on its other side. This is the world of twenty-first-century depression—a nihilistic vision of a glutted society sick of its own limitations and its infinite ability to objectify daily life, the body, and sexuality into, to use Heathfield's words, "the dead channel of late night TV."[7] *Starfucker* is a world of violation in which the personality is mistaken for the person, the actor for the action, where we too become implicated in such objectifications of Hollywood personae. It is a world of cold crassness, culminating in the realization that all the crudeness, whorishness, banality we can imagine is exactly that—our own imaginings reflected back to ourselves as pathetic fantasies mirroring our own highly *devolved* relationship to the world.

But perhaps the aggression to the audience is here misplaced, since in contemporary society fantasy most often is in fact *not* left to individuals to create and disseminate to the masses, but is rather *manufactured* as its own industry—what Oskar Negt and Alexander Kluge refer to as the "consciousness industry."[8]

Opportunity

Artists are those who see opportunity where others see mundanity. They are not afraid to make their own acquisitions, forgettings, and retrievals available to those who may be less willing to expose their projections or to live with the humiliation such disassembling can cause. Rosmarie Waldrop writes: "Writers we might say are those who engage in the act of replaying the erasures, of hearing the silence when spoken." Edmond Jabès writes: "voice? The history of silence is a text. Listening to silence, a book."[9]

Writing, painting, art making—"making a piece" of the whole—are all about following a pattern of thought, attempting to approach, as closely as one can, how one experiences the world outside as it interacts with the world inside. They are about speaking what has not as yet and may never be spoken, and moving the internal to the external within the parameters of a form.

Such forms are about developing a way to represent alternative consciousnesses—in Marx's sense, "to make the world aware of its own consciousness, in awakening it out of its dream about itself in explaining to it the meaning of its own actions."[10]

"One thought fills immensity," writes poet William Blake.[11] One thought leads to the next, to the next. It is the chronicling of this process as it develops and the perfecting of the representation of this chronicling with a sufficient degree of artifice that allow writing and art to communicate to an audience outside the self, the intention of the self to interpret the world.

This process can begin with a blank page, canvas, theater screen devoid of images, or a milky colored eighteenth-century wall with sealed gothic windows, opposite an overdesigned twenty-first-century hotel, on a side street, across a famous bridge, at the back of a great repository of the imagination, on a stormy day, in a city that sank ten inches in the past century, built and rebuilt on a dream, that, nonetheless, in this incarnation has miraculously resisted the *acqua alta,* the high water, that has threatened to reclaim, to vanish, to bury, to erase, to obliterate, to draw it back into its dark depths for centuries.

Notes

1. I wrote this chapter as a response to an unpublished piece by writer and critic Adrian Heathfield called "I Feel My Life a Movie I Never Saw." This process of writing in response to Heathfield is something we have done several times for the Goat Island performance company's Summer School. We call it "creative response." The title is a reference to the high water that swells in Venice at certain times of the year, threatening to take the city with it in its wake.

2. Wilhelm Reich, *The Murder of Christ: The Emotional Plague of Mankind* (New York: Farrar, Straus and Giroux, 1971).

3. Adrian Heathfield, "I Feel My Life a Movie I Never Saw," unpublished paper, School of the Art Institute of Chicago, Chicago, 2001.

4. Ibid.

5. Ibid.

6. Ibid.

7. Ibid.

8. Oskar Negt and Alexander Kluge, *Public Sphere and Experience: Toward an Analysis of the Bourgeois and Proletarian Public Sphere,* trans. Peter Labanyi and David Owen (Minneapolis: University of Minnesota Press, 1993).

9. Rosmarie Waldrop, *Lavish Absence: Recalling and Rereading Edmond Jabès* (Middletown, CT: Wesleyan University Press, 2002), 104.

10. Karl Marx, *Writings of the Young Marx on Philosophy and Society,* ed. Loyd D. Easton and Kurt H. Guddat (Garden City, NY: Doubleday, 1967), 214.

11. William Blake, "The Marriage of Heaven and Hell," in *Blake Complete Writings,* ed. Geoffrey Keynes (London: Oxford University Press, 1966), 151.

Index

❧

Page numbers in bold indicate photographs.

About the Author

⊰⊱

Carol Becker is Professor of the Arts and Dean of the School of the Arts at Columbia University. She is the author of several books and numerous articles on art, artists, pedagogy, and critical theory. Her previous books include *The Subversive Imagination: Artists, Society, and Social Responsibility* and *Surpassing the Spectacle: Global Transformations and the Changing Politics of Art.*